To learn more see: www.dansommer.biz

AIDCO

MARKETING

5 STEPS TO

BUSINESS

SUCCESS

By,

DAN SOMMER

Lulu.com

AIDCO Marketing - 5 Steps To Business Success

© 2010 by Dan Sommer. All rights reserved.

This book is designed to provide accurate and authoritative information in regard to the subject matter covered. It is sold with the understanding that the publisher is not engaged in rendering legal, accounting, or other professional service. If legal advice or expert assistance is required, the services of a competent professional person should be sought. *From a Declaration of Principles jointly adopted by a Committee of the American Bar Association and a Committee of Publishers.*

Author; Dan Sommer
Design & Layout by Dan Sommer
Published by Lulu.com
Printed by Lulu.com
ISBN Number: 978-0-557-40200-7

Fair Use Notice: This book contains some copyrighted photos, the use of which has not always been specifically authorized by the copyright owner. None of these photos has been used to advertise the book in any way; the author is only making such material available, in his efforts to advance the understanding of business marketing. The author believe this constitutes a 'fair use' of any such copyrighted photos, as provided for in section 107 of the US Copyright Law. In accordance with Title 17 U.S.C. Section 107.

A = Attention

I = Interest

D = Dominate

C = Confirm

O = Overcome

Dedicated to Ingunn,

The woman that I have loved for 25 years and who have taught me invaluable lessons about economics and finances.

www.DanSommer.Biz is the personal website of Dan Sommer; the founder of Dan Sommer Consulting, a Career Coaching & Business Consultancy. Dan is also a founding partner and Director of Global Executive Outreach Ltd, a UK risk and crisis management consultancy.

CONTENTS

Introduction   Page 9

Chapter 1: The AIDCO Power   Page 13

Chapter 2: A – for Advertise   Page 17

Chapter 3: I – for Inform   Page 65

Chapter 4: D – for Dominate   Page 79

Chapter 5: C – for Confirm   Page 89

Chapter 6: O – for Overcome   Page 97

Chapter 7: It's AIDCO Time   Page 109

Chapter 8: Dan Sommer   Page 127

Recommended Reading   Page 155

The AIDCO Marketing Manual by Dan Sommer

Introduction

A business plan is exactly what the words says, a plan! The plan can be the best-researched and well-founded plan ever, but that does not make it come through.

Without a straightforward, hard-ass marketing strategy and well planned sales campaigns, it will just be another plan. Just another plan, like so many before that failed to bring dreams to reality. Just another plan, which will at best most likely take years of frustrating hard work and tears to realize. But despair not for this is where AIDCO comes in to your rescue; and believe me AIDCO works. That's what I have proven the last years with my Security & Protection consultancy businesses.

Let me be honest with you, I did not learn this the easy way, and neither are you going to do. Success comes from "smart work" not just "hard work", I unfortunately had to learn that fact the hard way, through years of frustration and economical hardship, which almost drove me bankrupt!

I had developed one of the best training programs available to the private security sector. Big words, I will admit that… but I have trained law enforcement and security professionals from three continents, and they all agree, that my courses were highly advanced and one of the best, they had ever attended.

I had invested three years in the development and rewriting of my training textbooks and PowerPoint presentations. The practical lessons were based on my seventeen years in the security fields.

In spring 2000, I rewrote my business plan and by investing my lifesavings and after finding a business sponsor, I bought a small, but well-known European security training company, and consequently set out to conquer the private security training market. In the end of 2002, I had provided training in six countries, on three continents… and I was as broke as ever!

I had been working 16+ hours a day, never had time for my wife and three kids; and to add upon my troubles with the financial problems, my marriage was falling apart. During Christmas 2002, I was very alone in a far away country, frustrated, stressed and definitely in depression.

That's when I decided to change things!

Did business change? It changed a 180°! From spring 2003 until summer 2005, I studied and worked on marketing and sales methods, until my head would burst. In autumn 2005, I finally found success and every business deal I made after that left me with a significant profit, which led me on to further business deals.

From 2003 to 2006, I even sold five international franchises of my main business, three in Europe, one in Hong Kong and one in Mexico. During the same time span I successfully started and sold two security training companies, of which one was located in Iceland and the other in England.

In 2007 I finally reached success, and in 2009, I broke the USD $1,000,000.00 business threshold. How did I do it?

Well I am about to teach you that!

The AIDCO Marketing Manual by Dan Sommer

The AIDCO Power

True AIDCO power comes from using the AIDCO system, with an enterprising and innovative spirit. Although initially inspired by the A-I-D-C-A sales process (Attention, Interest, Desire, Conviction and Action).

I created AIDCO as a system for guiding your business planning and your personal and business marketing. If you are not familiar with the AIDCA sales process, then I explain it in detail in my manual *"The Modern Entrepreneur"*. For now, it is sufficient to say that AIDCA is a "sales tool" within the AIDCO plan.

A-I-D-C-O is my acronym for Advertising, Inform, Dominate, Confirm and Overcome. AIDCO also has a deeper meaning in the form of an AID-Company. That is my vision with AIDCO, to aid you on your way towards achieving success in your field of business.

This manual will help both the novice and the experienced entrepreneur, to succeed in small or big business. I know how difficult it is to start up an entrepreneurial business. If you follow the AIDCO process as laid out in this manual, you will be off to a much better start than I did.

The AIDCO system will power-lift your business to success if you have both courage and passion. Most of us have courage and passion; we just need a little support and encouragement in order to become successful...

That's why I created the AIDCO System!

Evolution Created Life, But

Revolution Create Business

Dan Sommer

For your entrepreneurial business to stand out in the crowd you need a highly motivated personal drive and you need to be revolutionary! Statistics shows that 96% of new entrepreneurs go out of business within 3 years. AIDCO will keep you among the 4%.

Of everything, I will teach you in this book; this is the most important factor for you to understand the fact; that if you and your business don't make a significant difference, you won't be around for long.

Let's repeat that: if you don't make a significant difference you won't be around for long!

Always keep your clients and your goals in your sights, never let either of them out of your sight or mind!

Be unique and innovative in your choice of products, and be different in your services. Be revolutionary and provocative in your marketing strategies, but do it without being blasphemous or insulting. In addition, you must be consistently professional and in line with your business or brand image.

This is it! This is the time and this is the place in your business career, where you will start to make a difference. Repeat that to yourself right now and do it with a loud cheer. This is you making a real difference in the world and you started today!

So take aim at your chosen clientele, give them all you got, and always keep your competitors in the rearview mirror. **It is AIDCO Time!**

Advertise

*In the beginning
was the word*

*And the word was
with Dan*

*And the word
was...*

AIDCO!

Did that catch your attention? Good, that is the purpose of any advertising, to catch the attention of your targeted customer group. If it did not catch your attention, then see Gospel of John 1:1.

If your advertisements are unique or provocative then customers will remember it, and they will also remember the business, product or brand advertised. It still comes as a *Surprise* to me, but new entrepreneurs often ask me this question:
"Do I need to advertise?"...

They often decide not to invest in advertising and support the decision with these arguments:

I have contacts through my previous careers!

It is just a small consultancy business!

I will just do phone calls and persuade!

Have you ever asked yourself this question and/or have you used these arguments in favor of not advertising? Well, I can tell you the correct answer right now; <u>YES, You Need to Advertise!</u>

Such *arguments* are only *objections* and even worse, they are lousy *objections*!

> ***"The business that considers itself immune to the necessity for advertising sooner or later finds itself immune to business."***
>
> *Derby Brown*

There is no success in business without advertising, that is the truth and no arguments or objections can change that fact. However, advertising can be many different things besides the "big-time ads": commercial TV ads, full-page ads in the newspapers, and radio advertising etc.

Pepsi is a typical example of the users of different and funny advertisings, which cost small fortunes to create and display.

This type of "big-time" advertising can be highly effective, however they are also outrageously expensive to produce and air. Expensive in such large cash amounts that the vast majority of entrepreneurs can only dream of affording them; especially in the first years of their businesses.

The "Lift Sharpen Up" TV ad is an excellent example of an ad that builds brand by amusing the viewer but without really selling anything. It is successful marketing that costs big bucks. If you haven't seen the ad, then go and watch it on YouTube!

If you can afford, those types of advertisings you don't need advice from me on this issue. Your consultants at the advertising agency will tell you all you need to know, as long as you have the cash…

However, if you cannot afford those types of advertising, then I can help you find excellent ways to advertise without spending your savings.

But, before we go into the more specific ways of advertising your small business, I want to tell you a few truths about advertising. I will also tell you why advertising is so important to your business and why it is, that without advertising you won't be around here much longer.

Your advertising campaign could and should have several specific purposes, such as:

- ✓ Creating customer awareness about your products and/or services
- ✓ Creating "Brand" recognition and a following.
- ✓ Provide information about your products and/or services
- ✓ Setting the "prize & image" for your products and/or services
- ✓ Entertain your targeted audience while still providing some or all of the information
- ✓ Directly selling your product or services.

Attention, an ad should only have one function, not two or three!

Your ad could be designed to:
- ✓ Getting prospects to visit your website, office or store.
- ✓ Getting prospects to call a "consultant or sales person.
- ✓ Designed to collect prospects contact details, in return for a gift etc.

Think about all the marketing campaigns that go on in the summertime; where you collect tokens in order to get a free product etc. That is brand promotion but when you submit your tokens, the business also collects your contact details.

Your prospects and existing customers contact details are <u>the most valuable asset</u> your business will ever have. Contact details equals access, and having access to your customers is fundamental to business success.

A Promotional-ad is designed solely to promote your brand or the image associated with your brand. A sales-ad is directly designed to sell a product or a service and must therefore first get your attention, instill a desire, make an offer and end with a direct call for action.

No matter what the ad is designed to do, it should be just one thing, or else the ad will lack focus and thus it will not provide the results hoped for. Yet, this is one of the most common mistakes made by unqualified advertising agencies. Such agencies are more focused on being nominated for an *"ad design award"*, than on actually helping your business succeed by increasing your sales.

Although the vast majority of prospects recognize advertising as a sales tool, they nevertheless subconsciously "judge" the business doing the advertising on several points:

- ✓ The average consumer mentally determines the standard of a specific product or a service; if it is not advertised, it isn't cool.

- ✓ The advertisement also gives the average consumer a trust in the "health" situation of a business; consumers perceive businesses that advertise as healthy businesses.

- ✓ The average consumer perceives the size of the advertising campaign as giving credence to the business that is advertising.

- ✓ The average consumer also perceives the cleverness of the advertising as an indicator of the quality of the advertised product and/or the service and skills of the business that is advertising.

✓ Branded ad's influence the average consumer more than non-branded advertising.

✓ The average consumer reacts highly positive to advertisings that are seen to be clever, original, humorous and more reflective of real life.

✓ So, advertise as often as you can afford and in as many diverse forms as you can imagine!

"Advertising is everything with a name or brand on it"

Tom Peters

Branding is a highly important point, far more so than any features or benefits. People averagely buy Nike shoes because they are Nike's, not because they were especially looking for the specific features or benefits that the specific Nike shoe gives them. The features and benefits are an important part of the overall product satisfaction, but many of the benefits are from the "prestige" and acceptance that comes from wearing Nike's.

JUST BECAUSE YOU'RE A NICE GIRL DOESN'T MEAN YOU CAN'T HAVE EVIL LEGS.

Notice that there is no specific product advertised in this ad; it's all about the NIKE brand and creating a desire!

Branding breeds trust and trust leads to a purchase; that's a fact in all business. Whether your business is about services or products, you need to establish your name or brand. That can only be done through repeated exposure of your name or brand. Look at the auto business, you don't see ads for a new model name, you see ads for a brand name and then the model name.

Always keep in mind that your brand is much more than just your product or service, it is part of every aspect of your product/s or service/s.

Keep the above quote in mind *"advertising is everything with a name or brand upon it"*. That means that all your marketing material is part of your advertising campaign. Such material includes everything with your company and brand name/s on it, including all personnel with a name tag, uniform or business card!

When meeting prospective clients, make sure your dress and appearance matches your company and brand image. And keep in mind that your *appearance* includes everything from your hair to your shoes, and your car etc. Make sure your performance also matches your company and brand image; this includes posture, language and how you greet your clients. This obviously applies to all of your company staff as well.

Brian Tracy is the master of selling his own talents, through both tangible and intangible services. He succeeds by always being professional from top to toe, and delivering exactly what he promises; himself and his successful tactics...

If your business is about selling a service such as consultancy services; then you cannot provide prospective clients with samples to see, feel or

I highly recommend you read and study his career success book "Focal Point"!

try, unless you give them a service for free. So <u>they will instead feel you out</u>... so you better look and behave as the image you want to project. Therefore, you have to ensure that your tangible marketing material instills trust in the minds of your prospective clients.

Thus all your marketing materials from your logo and letterhead to your brochures, websites and business cards, is the front line material "troops" for your advertising campaign.

Therefore, it is "crucial" that your marketing materials are of quality material and design, and show off the <u>professional appearance</u> your services demand. Make sure there are no "typos" or bad grammar unless that is part of your image, this includes all proposals etc.

Don't forget that the furniture, layout and look of your office and conference room, also have to match your image.

If your product or service does not have a feature that your competitor's products or services have, then use that to your advantage. Turn a <u>"negative" into a positive aspect</u>. This is an old sales tactic utilized successfully by the sales representatives working for Ford. When selling the Ford-T in the 1920's, one of their slogans was:

"You can have it in any color you want, as long as it is in black!"

That tactic is just as potent today as it was in the 1920's. It is in fact still a successful tactic for selling cars, and salesmen are today using this tactic to sell an inexpensive SUV brand, which does not have all the luxury features of its competing brands.

<u>Negative statements are immediately believed</u> by your customers when they are made by yourself. Because, now you have voluntarily emitted a fault, your customers will immediately believe you and now they will trust what else you say.

Land Rover Freelander's 2006 magazine *"Maasai ad"* is definitely a creative and different ad, which stands apart from other car ads.

Whenever you make a positive statement about yourself or your product, your prospects instantly become highly suspicious and want proof. No one asks for proof of a negative statement, they just assume it is true.

Thus a negative statement is an excellent opening paragraph in a sales letter or as an icebreaker in a conversation. However, a negative statement must be followed by a positive statement about the benefits you or your products provide instead.

Another very important point about your product or services versus the competitors is to use their faults to your advantage. But, be careful how you phrase it, because companies that slant their competitors are perceived as not having enough good to say about their own product or service. So to quote myself:

"Don't kick them while they are down... step on them"

Dan Sommer

That means that if your competitors product or service has a fault, then use it to your advantage. Not by mentioning their fault, but by mentioning that your product has a solution to that specific problem.

The customer will "see" your brand as the positive and see your competitor's product as the negative. They will mentally make a connection between the fault and your competitor, and connect your product with the solution. In marketing this is referred to as "hanging a negative" on competitors.

However, your new solution has to refer to a negative that prospects will immediately connect with your competitor. Thus the negative have to be based on a commonly perceived "truth".

This Pepsi ad makes a jokingly but negative statement about Mr. Right. But it also directly implies that through Pepsi Mr. Right gets the benefits of all Miss Sexy's features. Thus turning Negative into positive.

Always think about how you can use the features of your products or services, or the lack of features to make "it" and you appear unique.

Pepsi took on Coca Cola's century old product slogan "the original" and turned the Pepsi slogan into *"the choice of a new generation"*. Always present your products or services as the "New" alternative and don't be afraid to take on the Big Boys.

Look hard at your product, service or brand, and find at least one or two unique or different features. These features should be your primary focus when advertising your brand, products and/or services.

If your products don't offer anything unique, then either the product or your marketing team is crap!

Always fight for first place, not second or third! But keep in mind, that it is usually cold at the top, thus the companies with the largest market share also receives the most slander.

Using their position as the "runner up" in car rentals as a key point in their market plan, has paid off big time for Avis. Because customers perceive that the runner up are indeed more passionate and eager to please them than the industry leader!

Being the "upstart" in the second place, often mean higher profits and better reputation.

The car rental Avis have for years used their second runner up position, to appear better service minded than their larger competitor Hertz.

Thus Avis slogan has simply and effectively been *"we try harder"*. The slogan is believable as customers "know" that Avis are nr 2!

"Words tell,

Pictures sell"

Author Unknown

Successful advertisings provoke responses and make changes to people's perceptions. That "words tell and pictures sell" is a well known fact in modern day advertising.

Yet the reason a picture sell, is due to the fact that it easily grabs your attention.

However, copy writing and sales letters have found that pictures do not increase sales revenue. This is why most online sales "Guru's" websites often only includes one picture on the top and is followed up by lots of text describing benefits.

For a picture to be effective it must be relevant, but it does not necessarily have to show the product itself.

Because, it is more important to convey an image of what the product will offer the buyer.

The picture needs to convey positive feelings about what the product will do for the buyer, such as be beautiful, sexy and wealthy or live an exciting life, and or have more time for hobbies and pleasures etc.

Do you see any price, features or product details in this old Coca Cola advertising?

No! Well that is due to the fact that Coca Cola knows that benefits whether obvious or implied, are the key points in successful marketing.

Keep in mind that "the target of your ad" is usually not the same, as the market who will end up buying your product or service.

The ad on the next page is an example of this. Because, the image of the female Caucasian doctor, is not intended to market only to female Caucasian doctors.

In fact if your ad is designed to imply (the target) that the product or service is for the rich, successful or beautiful. Then those who desire to belong to a user group that is rich, successful or beautiful will want to buy the product or service.

Not quite the spitting image of your Doctor is she? Well that's because she conveys the benefit of sexual appeal to the client group. And who would not want to belong to a sexy client/user group?

This fact explains why non-athletes are drinking Gatorade or dressing in high-tech PUMA athletic training suits etc. Or why both mature people and the elderly also drinks Pepsi, even though it is the "Choice of a New Generation".

I hope you noticed how Pepsi brilliantly used the marketing strategy of "hanging a negative" on Coca Cola. By stating that Pepsi is the "choice of the new generation", then drinkers of Coca Cola, must logically belong to a user group consisting of conservative and old fashioned people.

To add to Pepsi's brilliant strategy then Coca Cola's statements of being the "original", "classic" or "the real cola" only goes to prove Pepsi's point.

What is she actually offering in this add?

Taste, flavor, or price... maybe... but is it only the Coke that is being offered?

The success factor here is that Coca Cola advertises the obvious and hidden benefits of their product!

So always focus your marketing on one "target group" that have an image that has a high appeal to your actual market group. Don't diversify your ads and marketing in order to reach every market group, because if you do you will lose focus and image and appeal to none. Stick to one chosen target group and other market groups will follow.

The goal of your marketing should be to point out the benefits of using the product or services and to provoke the following thoughts in your prospects:

- *How do I get that too?*
- *Will this work for me?*
- *Is that really possible?*
- *Who else has done it?*
- *Can they prove it?*
- *Will they accept me as a client or customer?*
- *How do I start?*

Pictures are one of the best ways to grab the attention of new buyers, who must then be either "sold" by the text or a salesperson. The purpose of the picture is thus to attract the attention of a prospect, who must then be made to take "some" action that will lead to a sale.

Actions, could be visiting your website, calling your service line, visiting your store, or sign up to receive further information or make a purchase etc. Having detailed customer lists with full contact details is one of the most important tools in marketing.

Generally your existing customers do not usually read or listen to the same sales text/talk more than twice. However, seeing your advertising picture again and again will remind your customer of your product and convey a positive feeling or image of belonging to a privileged user group.

So, the next time you see a Coca Cola advertising, stop and look at what *message* it really conveys to you. It is not about product details, service or price; it is all about conveying feelings. Thus, benefits are what your advertising picture should convey. So, convey to your buyer the "benefits" that he/she will get from using your product and how using the product will make him or her feel.

Your products "benefits" are a far more important "sales point" in your marketing, than your product features or service details. There should be no doubt in anyone's mind that Coca Cola has been and is among the best business products ever produced. The Coca Cola Company owes its success not to the taste, quality or ingredients of their product, but to the benefits and feelings conveyed in their marketing campaigns. Therefore, in marketing and advertising, Coca Cola is the undisputed King!

Thus all your advertising pictures, must convey feelings and focus on benefits in order to be effective. And they must differentiate from the other advertisings pictures; your customer is exposed to. Otherwise they will just disappear in the crowd.

How and Where to Advertise

As an entrepreneur, you will have to focus your advertising campaign on reaching the clientele that you are seeking as your customers.

That may sound very logical, but the fact is that many small businesses continue to advertise in standard newspapers, or online by the use of banner ads. These are just two examples of advertising that are a waste of time and money, when comparing costs versus sales.

Advertisings that are bigger, better and brighter are expensive, but differentiation is not. So keep that in mind, when choosing pictures for your ads and where to place the ads! Placing expensive ads in national newspapers or in the international magazines does not pay off for the small entrepreneur. Simply because, their distribution is aimed at a far too broad customer group. It is far better to advertise in local or category specific papers or even better in micro-niche magazines.

Photo I took in Hong Kong, when teaching there. Even if you do read Chinese, do you notice any specific add here? Which ad stands apart? Where is the ad differentiation?

Do you think these ads are really worth their cost?

Writing articles and submitting them to niche specific newspapers and online directories is basically free "Advertising" and in addition it gives you an opportunity to "Inform" prospects about you and to "Dominate" your niche and "Convince" them that you are the answer they have been looking for. And best of all the only cost is your time.

So, it is cost beneficial to write a short article and submitting it to content relevant newspapers and magazines. Do not neglect to submit your articles to online article directories; these directories will help distribute your articles for you for free. Article Directories such as: Buzzle.com, Article-Emporium.com, EzineArticles.com reaches thousands of readers worldwide, who are looking for the exact products or services that you offer. Otherwise they would not be reading your article.

Another great factor of online article directories is the fact that Google robots "crawls" them daily and index the articles found on them. Google's top favorite is EzineArticles.com so that should be your first choice for posting your articles.

Do some keyword research first and then choose related keywords and keyword sentences, as your article headlines. Very soon your article will rank in the top ten Google search for that sentence or search phrase. This way you get known as an expert and will have a worldwide market reach. You also get a good ranking in the search engines, and best of all it is all for free.

I have personally written and posted articles on these sites, which have been read by more than 25.000 readers in less than two months. And since articles posted at these websites are also distributed free to other article sites; then my articles are now available at 129 sites worldwide.

Many readers contact me for further information and many of them later become my customers. But most importantly, the articles gave me access to a much broader marketing group, and helped turn my name into a brand.

Writing articles is not as difficult as many believe it is; it is merely a task of getting your thoughts and ideas down on paper. Simply write about your field of expertise; all of us have loads of hard learned lessons and important experiences we can share with interested peers, colleagues and customers.

All three groups are highly important for your success, the first two groups can and will spread your name and knowledge to others, and the third group pays your salary and bills.

The best way is just to start writing without any editing or setup, just write from your mind and heart. Then edit, cut and paste the article as needed and then edit again; finally run a spell check and voila you have an article.

With time and experience you will get better and better. However, it pays to have a friend or colleagues read it over and give constructive criticism of both the content and form before you distribute it.

The most important aspect of writing articles, eBooks or books is the status of being an author. With the author status comes authority, as it is derived from the very same word. With authority come recognition and respect, and both of them lead to increasing sales and eventually to higher fees, prices and profit margin.

Another highly important aspect of writing articles and submitting them to online article directories is that it drives targeted traffic to your website. By providing article directories with quality content (articles) that eZine publishers can use in their news and on their web sites. Your name and website link will soon be all over the web, making your name a known brand and bringing you targeted traffic which will increase your sales.

Search engines such as Google love content rich sites and visit the article directories several times a day. Thus your article containing your website link will be indexed by Google in less than 48 hours. Best of all, your article will be indexed on a basis of your subject line.

Because, high ranking article directories will now have links from your resource box to your site. Then your site will rise in importance in the search engines. Whereas Buzzle receive more visitors daily than the other sites, then eZine-Articles are the site than Google place highest value in. So, to gain high Search Engine Rankings, then eZineArticles should always be your first choice for article submission.

Keep your articles between 700 and 900 words. Early on I erroneously thought that longer was better and wrote articles that were 3000 words long. However, most readers want to read articles quickly and many will just "skim read" it. If your article ends up being 2-3000 word long, then you should post it as two articles instead of one.

Keep the AIDCA process in mind when editing your article; make sure the description and headline catches the reader's attention, ensure that the first paragraph will interest the reader enough to keep him reading the rest.

The body should contain questions followed by partial answers in order to create a desire and curiosity. In the closing you should focus on convincing the reader that you are "the" niche expert. In your closing there should be a "non-sales sounding" but direct call to action, which should make the reader want to visit your website and/or contact you for further information.

The bottom of your article should include a so-called "resource box"; which basically contains your personal and/or business details in two to four lines. The resource box should contain a personal and/or company bio and encouragement for the reader to seek further information from you or your company, regarding the topic of the article.

Thus articles covering different subjects should have different texts in the resource box!

Here is 5 hard-learned points of what not to do, when writing or posting an article:

1. Don't make it one of those self advertising, "BS full of hype" articles, that many amateurs post in the beginning. Believe me; it will only hurt your reputation. Keep the article interesting, factual and with relevant content worth reading.

2. Don't write a "sales-letter" type article, this is not what the article directories or their readers are looking for. Most likely your article will either be rejected or ignored.

3. Make sure you spell check your article, at least twice and preferably print it, and then read it on paper the following day. You will be amazed how much more you want to edit your article the day after.

4. Always edit it twice, with a full day between. Believe me, it is very embarrassing to receive emails commenting on your poor writing skills, just because you forgot to spell check and re-edit.

5. There should not be any links to your site or any affiliate sites in the body of the article, limit all links to the resource box. Some article directories will reject articles with links in the body text.

These are 5 points that I have learned the hard way. I have had to re-edit articles after initially releasing them. I have once been embarrassed by a poorly spelled article that I wrote in a rush and posted it on a news site. The article circulated the www for a full week before I could re-edit it.

Remember, that an article is a statement and your brand and business image, is polished or tainted by everything you do, say or publish!

Press Releases

Alternatively to writing articles, you can and should write press releases, also known as news statements or media releases. Send them to all niche relevant TV and Radio stations, newspapers, magazines and online news sites. Think of press releases as way to promote yourself and your business/brand in a low cost, but attention grapping manner. Press releases add credibility to your business, increases publicity and is free advertising. A press release is simply a story about your "newest" business achievement.

News desks at offline and online newspapers, TV and Radio stations, want and needs fresh news, trends, facts, statistics, researches, business ventures and interesting topics, which connects with your person, business or products. Your PR content should in addition to being newsworthy also be interesting, educational, inspirational, motivational and relevant to their subscribers.

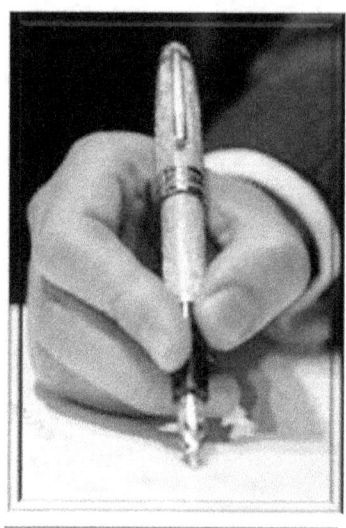

Getting on a local television or radio talk show with thousands of viewers or listeners, easily equal thousands of $ spend on advertising. And, it offers instant credibility for you and your business.

Any personal or business marketing plan etc are incomplete without Press Releases. Therefore all marketing plans should utilize press releases as a regular part of the full marketing strategy.

So, you should send out press releases when you establish your business and whenever you create or add a new product or service. You should also use it whenever your business or a staff member wins an award, or when you secure a large or important contract.

Whatever the reason, press releases should always be "newsworthy" to the news agencies that you submit them too. You should also post your press releases on your websites as this builds credibility and it is "believable" advertising. Because, press releases add credibility to your business and are an important tool in your business promotion.

Press releases are also often used by journalists who use them as an angle for an article. They will usually also want to interview you in relation to their article and this is some of the best advertising you can get. Again the best about this is that it is free and believable advertising.

Writing a press release is not rocket science. It is one of those marketing tasks, which with a little practice you can easily do yourself in less than two hours with my "Press Release Pro" wizard. Press releases needs to follow a simple setup and should contain the following elements:

Headline; A short attention grapping headline of about ten words, make it a news line not a sales line. Rewrite it until it sounds right and are catching, the headline is the most important part of your press release.

Capitalize the first letter of all words in the headline (except: "a", "an", "the", or prepositions such as "of", "to", or "from") etc.

The PressReleasePro is a press release package containing my own PRP software, a PR Manual and my PR sample. To learn more about the package visite my website:

www.dansommer.biz

Dateline and Name; The place you are sending your news release from, the date of the release and your name. It is a simple format: City, state, province, country, date and contact person. The dateline is usually "for immediate release". But if you plan to use your press release as part of a marketing campaign, or to coincide with another major event, then you can specify a set date such as "December 25, 2007" or "Valentine's Day" etc.

Lead Paragraph; Simply a summarization of your press release in max 2-5 sentences. Include all the basic information of the story here. Make it interesting, as it is usually all that is read by editors before they make the decision to print it or not. Confirm your lead paragraph's "key points" by including a few bullet point one-liners.

Graphic and/or Mediafile; most but not all Medias offer the opportunity to have a photo or logo included in the press release. Graphics are good for catching the readers' attention and it is more free advertising. Use a professional portrait photo of you or your business logo. The media you are addressing determines if it should be in color or in black and white. Some Medias also offers the opportunity to include relevant graphics such as product photo, graphs, product schematics and urls to media files such as voice or video etc.

PR Message; Use short sentences and include power words, but avoid "sales hype". Remember that it is a press release not a sales letter. Keep it in the one page range with maximum 400 words, and break it into paragraphs. Include all relevant information about you, your business, products or services. Explain the benefits that your product, service or business offers. Be specific! Direct the message in your press release at the reader group you are addressing, such as your target and/or market base, book publishers or investors etc. Ensure that your "most important" message is in the beginning of the text. So in case your content is cut short by an editor, you will not lose important parts of your press release information.

Closing Paragraph; Repeat your product, service or business details, the benefits it provides for your customers and all relevant dates. Include one or two pre-approved testimonials or quotes from satisfied customers and positive statements from "industry expert/s" etc. This is where you "convince" the editor that your press release is relevant and indeed news worthy.

Business History; A few sentences about you or your business, include the full business name, certifications, permits and associations etc.

Call For Action; This is your last chance to make a call for action on behalf of the reader. Directly instruct the reader to contact you to inquire further about the topic of your press release, and to receive further free and relevant information.

Business Details; Your call for action should be followed by your full business contact details such as: business name, postal address, contact name, title, phone and fax nr (use toll free if you have them and Skype number etc), email addresses and website links; the more contact options you offer to readers, the broader your reach will be.

The fact is that many readers/customers prefer to visit a website or to email their inquiry rather than to call, because they fear they will be directed to a sales person and "sold" if they do.

Banner Ads & Pay-per-Click

The traditional banner ads effectiveness have been dead and useless the last five years, and believe me they will not come back!

The only ones, who advocate these advertising methods, are those who sell them and that are usually poorly-performing internet sites. The problem with banner ads is that you can never just advertise, to your specific market niche.

There are thus very few professional sites that offers banner ads space. However, there are two very effective uses of banner ads.

1. The first is by using product specific banner ads within your own website, for cross promoting your products or services.

2. The second is by using attention catching banner ads on heavy traffic sites to create brand recognition among a wide audience.

Displaying your banner ads on heavy traffic sites to create brand awareness is very costly in the short term, but can bring significant gain in the long term.

Such ads should just promote your name or brand, not any specific services or products.

The less information the banner provides, the more curious it will make viewers, and thus the name or brand will be subconsciously remembered.

Pay Per Click Marketing

"Pay per click" or "click for points" are equally useless marketing tools, when comparing cost versus sales.

The only pay per click advertising that really pays off is Google's pay-per-click service; but even Google can be a big loss unless you do extensive keyword research before and carefully choose your keywords and phrases.

For a complete PPC Guide of how to make successful PPC ads; read my 2007 manual on Tactical PPC Marketing. See more on:

www.dansommer.biz

Doing some serious research into which keywords and phrases to bid on will save you big money.

However, one of the upsides of PPC marketing is that you can in effect target your competitors name or brand in your PPC campaign. For an example of this just go to google.com and search for Adobe Reader or Adobe Writer; you will quickly see that every newcomer and upstart in the PDF software market are directly targeting their PPC campaigns to the Adobe brand name.

Thus, whenever a consumer is looking for the Adobe PDF product, he is exposed to competing adds from alternative PDF software producers.

Websites

Your website is one of the most important advertising and marketing tools you will have, so do not neglect it. However, let me start by correcting a few misconceptions:

Build a website and start earning money...

Wrong, it has to be the right type of site, with the right layout and the right language suiting the type of customers you are targeting. Otherwise it is worthless.

Customers will find my site through Google...

Wrong, without the correct "HTML text" for SEO optimization, rich content, simple site navigation, search engine submissions, link ranking, "Google Ad sense ads" and popularity, it will not get a high Google search rank. My personal experience is that it is far easier to get a high rank on Yahoo than on Google. However Google is the "number one" search engine, so work it! The first thing you need nowadays is a

Google site map, if you don't have it then get it at www.sitemapbuilder.net

Having a high Hit ratio will ensure success...

Wrong, it is not the amount of hits or visits that will earn you money, (unless that is your marketing point); it is the ratio of hits/visits versus purchases that earns you money. You don't earn unless your visitor feels compelled to buy.

Once a visitor reads my site he will buy...

Wrong, market research indicates that more than 60% of prospects will not buy the first time they see or are exposed to a product or service. In online marketing these figures are even worse, just ask yourself: how many times have you visited sales websites without buying anything?

Fancy Flash sites & sounds attract visitors...

Wrong, it has been proven time and time again that the online customers want to see and read right away; they are searching for something and they don't have time for super Flash-sites and intro movies. You have only a few seconds to attract their attention toward your product or service; don't waste your prospects time. The only ones that promote flash designs and intro movies are website designers looking to earn extra money from YOU!

Graphics & savvy descriptions make sales...

Wrong, your business could be totally unknown to your new visitors. These potential customers can't touch, view, test or feel your products or services; therefore they cannot fully convince themselves that your product or service is worth their money.

The only way they can be convinced about the quality of your product or service, is if they take a chance and buy it... well that does happen, but just not that often that it can sustain your business! So you need to convince them in another way and that is by building trust between you and them.

This is best done by giving them an option to sign up for your free email newsletter, where you will be able to gain their trust with repeated quality newsletters.

One of the best auto-responder sites for collecting your prospects email address off your website and provide immediate information is aweber.com. This is the service I use personally.

Online Trust Issues

"A Boston Consulting Group; Consumer Survey found that 70% of respondents worry about making purchases online."

How many times have you been interested in an online product but have hesitated because you did not trust the company? I bet it has been quite often; so write your site in a manner that would make you buy. Ask yourself; what is it that make me suspicious when I read a sales ad? Then quickly remove such "components" from your website, and then you will be more likely to inspire trust and thus increase sales.

The Five Pillars of a Successful Ad Layout

Your ad must follow the Five-Steps of AIDCA – Attention, Interest, Desire, Conviction and Action. You should design your ad layout with those Five key points as the leading points for your Five Pillars of successful ad design.

AIDCA & the Five Pillars of Layout

1. Attention   ~ Photo-Visual-Graphic
2. Interest ~ Photo Caption and Headline
3. Desire ~ Sales Copy / text
4. Conviction   ~   Copy   Closing   / Testimonial
5. Action ~ Call for Action & Contact Details

Pillar 1 = Attention! Place your Attention Grabbing Photo-Graphic or Logo Here

Pillar 2 = Interest! Insert your Photo or Graphic Caption Description or use a Catching Headline

Pillar 3 = Desire! Your Sales Copy Text Here! Keep it focused on describing the benefits derived from your using your product or services and how each feature connects with one or several extra benefits.

Include Bullets with key benefits.
Benefit 1
Benefit 2
Benefit 3

Use Sub-Headlines
Use bold and italic and short paragraphs with direct sentences avoiding passive speech.
Key Feature
Key Feature

Your Closing Copy Sales Text is here in your last paragraph or sentence etc.

Pillar 4 = Conviction! Your Convincing testimonial from a happy client or niche expert.

Include Photo, Name, Address, Website etc. The more details the better, as it makes it convincing, real and very believable. In short make it Convincing.

Pillar 5 = Action! This is your Call For Action, use something like a "Limited supply or limited purchase time" etc. Or use a Coupon Form or request Specific Contact Details etc and name of advertiser and include an offer or special deal etc

In short, whether your ad is printed in Full-Page, Half-Page or Quarter-Page etc, the layout should always be based upon the Five Pillars of successful ad layout. However, if you are using Full-Page ads or Half-Page ads in landscape mode then you should use 2 or even 3 columns for your Copy Text.

Think *Magazine* style; narrow columns are easier and faster to read than wide or full page lines… Think *Pocketbooks!* Why do you think that the pocketbooks we all like to read in bed are all relatively narrow pages of text printed on yellowish non-glare paper? Yep, because it is easier to read!

Using AIDCA in the Ad Layout sequence:

- ✓ Pillar 1: is meant to catch the Attention of the reader or prospect and stop them from web browsing or page flipping in a magazine etc.

- ✓ Pillar 2: is meant to follow up the initial attention by providing a descriptive caption and a headline text, which will stir the curiosity of the reader or browser and make them read the copy text of the ad because their interest have been activated.

- ✓ Pillar 3: is meant to build upon the interest by pulling the reader into the copy sales text, by creating a desire in the reader for reaping the benefits that the product or service provides the user or users etc.

✓ Pillar 4: is meant to convince the reader that he or she is safe and secure in making the purchase and that it is not a "cat in the bag" offer. By now the reader's attention has been caught, his interest stirred and a desire awakened, and finally his last skeptical suspicions are evaporated by convincing him it is a safe and secure purchase.

✓ Pillar 5: is meant to pull the reader to take the action that the ad was designed to do, such as purchase a product, order a service or sign up for a mail list or membership etc.

The Ten Commandments of Ad Designing

1. Determine the purpose and function of the ad; what is it supposed to do? Is it brand advertising, direct sales or an action call etc? To ensure success then your ad should have one function only; you can always follow it up with another ad or a sales letter etc.

2. Catch Attention by using a photo or visual text that's catchy and Relevant to the product or

service. The photo should preferably show the benefits of using the product or enjoying the service etc, or show the product or service in its natural use.

3. Complete the photo or visual with a caption that explains the photo/visual to further sink in the message. Make sure the caption also indentifies any persons seen in the photo.

4. Interest the reader or viewer by using a strong headline, which should seek to answer reader questions such as: why do I care? What is in it for me? And why are you addressing me?

5. Create a smooth and simple layout of the ad, the safest bet is to follow the tried and tested "Z Layout" form and ensure that all components i.e. fonts, graphics and boxes are in symmetry and colors are themed.

6. Connect graphics and paragraphs by using Drop caps to draw the reader along your "story" set up. Ensure that drop cap style, font and color are in symmetry with the ad color theme.

7. Design and formulate your sales text on the benefits from using your product or service. For maximum effectiveness then make sure that the benefits that are described and "sold" in the sales copy text, is the same as are used in the headline.

8. Testimonials are the best argument for convincing the reader that what you are offering is worth the investment you are asking. So use testimonials and case studies or example stories to "backup" your "selling" benefits.

9. Guarantee your statements and promises with an actual guarantee. Always include some form of guarantee of usability as well as a guarantee for full replacement, repair, service or refunding etc. Keep in mind that experience have proven that a "Two point" guarantee is far better for sales than a "One point" guarantee etc.

10. Make an explicit and direct call for Action and to ensure it is taken seriously then include a set deadline and a "penalty" for failing to take action right now. This could mean limited availability or a significant price increase after the deadline expires. There must be an

incentive for making a fast response. Include as many contact or order methods as possible but ensure they are simple to use.

If you continuously and slavishly follow the Five Pillars of ad layout and adhere to the Five Points of AIDCA advertising, then you will continuously experience increased sales and profits.

It is very important point that you quickly realize that what you really need to run a profitable business is increasing sales and increasing income. All the other points that you are being told and sold… is secondary to the importance of increased sales and increased profits. And the best way to ensure increased sales and increased profits is marketing, and marketing is best done through advertising.

Another important point is that whether or not your ads will win a prize for being the most innovative or artistic ad etc, is irrelevant to your bottom line of profits. So, keep that fact in mind when the ad agency cooks up some new and fancy ad idea!

Advertising Campaigns

Don't despair because you feel that your recent advertising campaign isn't paying off; the fact is that even controversial advertising takes time to affect sales. Advertising isn't just about increasing your sales; it is just as much about establishing your name, service or brand.

"We find that advertising works the way the grass grows. You can never see it, but every week you have to mow the lawn."

Andy Tarshis

This is a quote I can personally vote for. I am never quite sure where my customers originally came to think of me or found my name or services, but the fact is the numbers keep increasing.

Of course you could and should ask your customers questions about where and how they came to know of your product or services. You can choose to either do it informally or provide new customers with a readymade questionnaire; this will help you determine which advertisements are paying off and which are not.

The truth is that you best customer for your new service or product is your existing customer. The first sales are always the hardest, the second sales are so much easier and after the third sale it is like cutting butter with a hot knife. Far too many businesses forget their existing customers and chase new ones like headless fools. Don't make the mistake of neglecting your existing customers, present to them first and ask them first.

Just remember to make it worth your customer's time to fill out the questionnaire; give them a small gift or discount etc. Simply show your appreciation for their effort and they will pay you back many times.

"Early to bed, early to rise, work like hell and advertise. "

Ted Turner

Well these words come from one of the modern business world's leading marketing experts; so there must be some truth in them. This man has managed to make his own name an internationally known brand and his products and services are well known all over the world. That's a feat only the really successful will ever accomplish. So, take heed of his words, unless of course you are a so-called "B" person like me, who is most creative after midnight. :-)

However; if you are a "B" person like me then you will simply have to change the quote to; "late to bed and late to rise, work like hell and advertise". It doesn't sound as good, but it's the results that matter not the rhyming.

If you like I are in the "B" type personality, then you are much more creative in the evening, and thus you need to use that time for doing creative tasks. Luckily for me, then my coaching and consultancy services cater to an international clientele.

So even though I start late, I still have time for the European afternoon business. As the European offices close then the American's open their offices and I can then work with that market until evening. Before I call it a "day" I catch the first hours of Asia's morning business.

So for me having a B-Type bio-clock actually helps me attract international clients, which in turn means I have access to a much larger group of prospects than if I just worked 9-5 and only marketed locally. Thus, as you can see, then there are business opportunities everywhere.

Inform

"Evolution creates life, but revolution creates business"

Dan Sommer

Information marketing is one of the most effective ways of "spreading the word" about you and your business. Use this type of marketing whenever you can, it is cheap, often free and carries far more weight than standard advertising.

This is because when you "inform" someone in a positive way about your product or service, that someone will tell someone else. That person perceives the information received from "second-hand" as more truthful and reliable than if he just heard it from you. It is word of mouth referral, one of the best marketing strategies available.

So jump start your word-of-mouth marketing campaign, by joining local and national business associations; such as clubs like Lions or Rex Rotary etc. Attend conferences, whether you intend to have a sales booth or not and do not limit your conference attendances only to conferences directly related to your business. Make sure you also attend the conferences that relate to your customer's businesses.

Whether you are attending an event in an association, club or at a conference, make good use of the lunch and coffee breaks by mingling with your peers and potential prospects.

Resist the urge to try to "sell" your products or services at these events. Instead you should focus on asking questions, listen and provide information only. But do hand out your business card and collect as many cards in return as you can, these are an excellent source for prospecting through follow up.

Above all, always be "positively minded" in all conversations, listen to what your peers have to say and ask plenty of questions. There is no-one we trust more or feel more positive about, than the person who shows interest in us and listen to our opinions. That person should be you!

Sowing an Idea

One of the best ways to "sell" (read inform) potential prospects, about your product or services, is by "casually" presenting your product or service as an idea. An idea of how you could help your peers solve some of their problems.

People are much more positively inclined to agree to an "idea", than to any sales pitch no matter how good and rehearsed it is.

The sales problem is the fact that if you present a product or service with too much enthusiasm, you often trigger a natural resistance, which soon becomes ego-based. This will near always "block" the sales progress and the deal runs out in the sand.

So by being subtle and presenting your product or service, as an idea during a conversation. You will receive a much more positive response, than by enthusiastically introducing *your* product or service, as the solution to your peer's problems.

Be patient and remember to listen well and show interest in your prospects life and business, so the conversation will leave them with both a pleasant experience and as well as a positive opinion about you and your business. Ideas generally need three full days (72 hours), to seep through the average person's "mental blocks" towards new ideas.

So remember to catch up with your prospect after the three to four days. Send them a genuine "thank you message" for the interesting conversation we had during the conference last weekend etc. Use e-mail or even better a personal hand written letter or alternatively make a call.

If you make a call; make sure it is not perceived as a sales pitch. Be genuine and ask for "clarification" about some point or a problem that came up in you conversation. Tell the person you are looking for his advice, on how to solve a similar problem you are having. This will flatter the prospect and as he has already mentally debated the "idea", you sowed in his mind. He will be interested in further discussions about trying your product or service.

> ## *"Man's mind, once stretched by a new idea, never regains its original dimensions."*
> *Oliver Wendell Holmes*

This ensures that your prospect will be positively inclined to receive your actual sales drive, as the prospect will already have mentally debated the "pros and cons" of your idea. Thus the following sale will usually be a smooth process.

Communication

One of the most neglected areas of marketing is something as plain and simple as good old-fashioned communication. Why do you think a business would decide to change its suppliers of products and services?

Do you think it is because they got a better offer?

Do you think it is because they were exposed to competitive advertising or a smooth sales representative?

Do you think it is because they found superior product or service elsewhere?

Do you think it is because they are unhappy with the delivery?

Do you think it is because they want to try another product or service?

Well then you are wrong, wrong, wrong… all the answers are usually wrong! Seventy percent (70%) changes their suppliers of product or services, because there were a direct lack of communication between the supplier and the buyer. A recent research by Forum Corporation, found that 70% of businesses changed suppliers because of a lack of communication!

The two other major reasons were: price 15% and quality 15%. Both of those I can assure you are usually also due to a lack of communication. If your customer changes supplier due to price, it is near always because you did not negotiate well enough and did not communicate the benefits.

If they changed supplier due to a lack of quality, it is because you did not communicate effectively and openly enough, to find out about the faults in time to correct them, or you did not explain the proper use of the product or service.

Good quality is no longer a competitive strength; today it is an expected requirement by customers. You won't keep your clients business, solely by offering good quality. But you will lose them in an instant, if you don't provide it!

If a customer changed supplier due to price, then you can be sure it is only half the story. Price is only an issue when the customer can't see or perceive the value of the product; so again it comes down to communication.

Be aware that low price is not a competitive edge. Because, there is always someone who will drop their prices further.

Take a look around you at any business niche, and you will near always find that the business who charge the highest prices, are also the one that makes the highest profits and have the largest market share.

Key point to notice; the businesses who charges the highest prices, are also the one that makes the highest profits and have the largest market share.

Customers do not like to complain, so you need to ask questions about their satisfaction level and to get honest answers, you will first have to establish close rapport and trust with your customers.

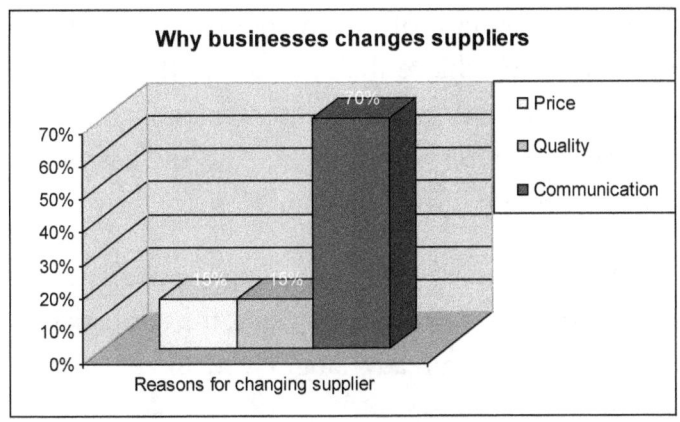

Info Marketing is Key to Your Success

"Infomarketing" as it is known today is essentially marketing through providing your targeted niche prospects and customers with niche specific information that they crave and need. As you provide them with free knowledge in form of articles, newsletters and video tutorials you are also establishing yourself as an expert in their mind, and you can market your fee-based products or services at the same time.

Giving away free but valuable information may initially seem like bad business, and in some ways it is; that is if you look at it as business. Because, it is not business it is marketing, and the most efficient form of marketing.

Near all of the "Gurus" or "Experts" you find in every industry or niche, have reached their status through the strategy of infomarketing. Thus, if you want or need to achieve the same status then you need to do what they did… and that is to market yourself as the "guru or expert" in your field. And the best way to do that is through infomarketing.

Write articles and use email newsletters to establish yourself as an expert, using the strategies and tactics that I have already taught you in the *Advertise Chapter*.

Social Sites & Infomarketing

Another key point for your AIDCO marketing campaign is to take full advantage of free Social Sites in your marketing. Social Sites and/or Social Networks, like Myspace, Facebook, linkedin and Squidoo etc...are a great way to get your ideas and products in front of a huge market of prospects.

Most (if not all) of these sites, allow you to create a "profile" that everyone can see and locate through search engines. Inside that profile, you can and should "carefully" direct your traffic to either your main website or direct them to a number of options that leads to your products and services sales sites.

For an extensive list of the major Social Sites and Social Networks and their page ranks, see my 2008 Social Site Marketing Directory.

Just visit my website :

www.dansommer.biz

I would suggest that you interact with the social networks and offer "free information" that is designed to gently push your traffic towards your main websites and sales sites.

Most of the social sites have very high Google page ranks and sites with a page rank of 6 or more are indexed daily by the search engines for new and fresh content.

Sites with a page rank of 8 or more are indexed dozens of times per day. Thus your postings on these sites can get your informational piece and your included website link indexed by Google in 30 minutes or less! Social sites are experiencing the highest number of visits per day and keep visitors for the longest time as well. So do not neglect them in your marketing campaign.

Website Video Marketing

By activating both the senses of sight and sound in a combination with short textual messages, web video can and will (if used right) boost both your online and offline sales. Because, the added communication between you and your website visitors, will enhance your visitor's experience and increase "customer trust", which leads to higher sales volume and better visitor conversion rates.

A web video does not have to be a "direct" sales video, but can also be footage taken of third party environments to which a narration has been added, to footage of private life or family vacations, and yet still positively increase online sales rates. It all depends on the specific websites "relationship" with their online visitors / viewers and how many of them are within your prospect group or among your current customers.

In other words, the type of web video you can and/or should use depends solely on the type of relationship you have or wish to have, with your viewers and customers. If you really wants to boost your sales volume and profits then nothing will do that better than a video demonstration of your product or service in action; if you should have any doubts about that statement, then turn on your television and flick to a infomercial sales channel.

For a complete guide to how to successfully market your business with website videos, see my 2008 MBA Website Video Success Manual on my website:

www.dansommer.biz

It is a fact that more sales volume and profits have been brought in by televised infomercials than by any other sales methods. However, airing your sales video on an infomercial channel is highly expensive, whereas adding your home made sales video to your website will cost you from $0 to $500.

Make your website videos yourself and narrate them with your own voice to increase perceived customer interaction with you. Remember that website videos are not expected to be of the same quality as Hollywood movies, nor have loads of special effects. Keep them small in size for quick downloading and keep them short and around Five minutes in length.

The best format is Flash, because it offers excellent compatibility and the "file size output" is just a little bit bigger than similar-quality video in other formats.

Your video should preferably be differentiating and unique. Unique means that the viewer will think it is both new and covers something new or a different angle on a known subject. When it is new and unique, then it will make your viewers want to watch it and pay attention to your video message.

If your video is stale and seems to be rehashed information, which the viewer have often heard or seen before, then the viewer is simply going to move on. This is a key point in the making and breaking of your videos success with generating new customers or clients for you.

Once your video is complete, make sure that you have included a direct call to action in your video. You will need to "tactfully" ask the viewer to do something. This can be suggesting that for more information they visit your website, they call you to get started, or contact for a free commercial.

Avoid the following

- ✓ Stripes and other detailed patterns as they will make your video look corny
- ✓ Wide shots with too many objects or details and trees and other complicated and patterned matter
- ✓ Excessive of camera movements and repeated zooming from and back
- ✓ Quick or erratic movement of persons or objects in the video as this demand more viewer concentration and cause viewer fatigue and eye strain
- ✓ High-contrast lighting such as having both shadow and sunlight visible in the same video frame
- ✓ "Hot spots" such as small areas of bright lights or sunlit windows

- ✓ Videos with a "talking head" are bad for online viewer retention, research shows that in just 24 seconds, online viewers lose interest in such videos
- ✓ Avoid unnecessary objects in the video as they distract viewer attention
- ✓ Avoid having distracting objects on your website in direct view of the video
- ✓ Research shows that viewers will repeatedly glance to the left or right of the video while watching it. So ensure any objects there are relevant to the message in your video

Dominate

"Good businesses are evolutionary,

Great businesses are revolutionary"

Dan Sommer

It is hard work to be successful in one market niche; it is near impossible to be successful in two or three market niches. Therefore, you should stay with the basics and focus your marketing on <u>the niche wherein you are unique</u>. To effectively dominate a market niche, not just today but in the future as well, you will need to be innovative and differential in your products or services.

No business survives on past fame, if you are not en-route to the top today, you will be at the bottom tomorrow. Extreme…yes! But it is the truth in today's competitive business world. Your <u>customers need to gain</u> from buying from you, if they don't they will soon look elsewhere with their purchases.

In today's world; getting gain is not necessarily from buying or having the best product, it often come from buying or having the newest product. To provide your customers with that gain, you will need to offer them something new. The most important marketing point your business can ever have is to be the "Niche" leader in a category. Because, it is always better to be first brand in a category than having a better product or service.

I dominate the Google search engine for my name and / or term "Dan Sommer"; in fact I hold 7 of the top 10 rankings and best of all I hold the top 3 ranks!

In short that is personal marketing at its best.

Where do you rank on Google? If you are not in the Top 10 then you need to AIDCO up your marketing!

This is due to the fact that even though if we all love to talk about change; in reality people resist changes in their life's and this is most often a subconscious action. Thus customers stick with their brand and that is the brand they know; rather than go and try something new. This count for all categories, fields or niches you are doing business in.

To be first in a category all you need to do is to create a new and innovative product prototype, then market and sell it. Now just let your competitors work on improving it, and while they do that, you create and launch a new prototype. This way you will always be known as the leader and your competitors as the copy-cats.

Prototype Development Plan

To stay ahead and be on the edge of your marketing niche, you need to be "the" one business that creates the trends.

This is not as hard as it sounds, it is only a question of skills and will power; abilities you already have.

Because if you did not have them, you would not be an entrepreneur and would not be the type that would buy and read this book.

But you are reading it, so the truth is that you are clearly an entrepreneur in spirit and action!

"If it doesn't sell, it isn't creative"

David Ogilvy

In todays competitive business world, many cutting-edge fortune 500 companies have been forced to reconstruct their former business strategies. They are now enbracing innovation in order to avoid stagnation. As an entrepreneur you have to do the same, otherwise you wont be around for long.

I have included a skeleton-guideline for how to start your prototype development plan; I have used this plan successfully in my own business and with my clients. The plan is similar to the ones used in fortune 500 companies and was first designed by Tom Peters "the guru" of business innovation.

Fortune-500 - Rapid Development Plan

1. Create a new innovative idea for your business

2. Collect all "free" materials related to the idea

3. Set a short time frame in days or weeks not months, in which to optain your prototype

4. Select a primary and secondary market to test your prototype on

5. Select a marketing campaign best suited to target the markets with

6. Launch your prototype at your primary market

7. Analyze the results in days, not weeks

8. Correct any discovered faults in both design and marketing method, quickly in days not weeks

9. Relaunch at the secondary market

10. If successful, reap the profits and goto (12)

11. If unsuccessful, forget the idea and accept the loss (it where minimal) and proceed to 13

12. Make a postitive marketing plan and "sell" it to the company CEO or EO of the Production department. Alternatively sell to the highest outside bidder; quickly!

13. "Create a new innovative idea for your business"

Follow the above Fortune-500 development plan continuously, and I can guarantee you that your competitors will never catch up with you.

Within a year or two, you will be the business everyone talks about and the big players will try to either recruit you or hire you as an outside Expert-Consultant. Either way you will retain a high income that ensures, you will achieve your goals.

Detailed Fortune-500 Development Plan

Creating an "Idea" which is truly a brilliant idea, is unfortunately not an easy thing to do for most people. Because, the majority of ideas that come into people's heads are neither very good nor executable. The classic mistake is to think that what you like is what other people like and that your "improved product" is what everyone wants.

What you should do is: <u>First determine your skills</u> and then your company's skills and then go on from there. Start with something you know something about, but ensure it is something for which there is a <u>sustainable market available</u> and preferably an existing market.

Sit your "team/s" down tell everyone to come back in two days with five new ideas each.

After two days have a brainstorming meeting where each team member presents one idea at a time and the rest of the team criticize it. Each team member should present only one idea at a time and then answer questions and partake in the criticism of the idea. Then the next team member brings an idea up for review.

> ## *"It takes courage to be creative. Just as soon as you have a new idea, you are a minority of one. "*
>
> *E. Paul Torrance*

If you ask each person to present their five ideas consecutively; the criticism of the person's ideas will often be too much for the person to take. His motivation will drop and he will be overly negative (revengeful) when faced with other member's ideas.

The fact is that most ideas, only seems good when we get them, upon thorough contemplation 99% are faulty, useless or totally unrealistic.

However, to be ahead in today's business world you need to be ruthlessly innovative, in both your creation of products or services and in your ways of marketing.

The following is a metaphorical story, I like to tell business people, to get them to comprehend the ruthlessness of modern business innovation.

"Give birth to a son, train him to be a soldier and teach him to kill. Set him loose upon your enemies and reap the spoils of war. When he stops to catch his breath, kill him... and bring forth your second son!"

Many business-persons will balk and object at the innovation process and say; we cannot afford to be failing in our developments, our economy and reputation will not survive it!

"The best way to get a good idea, is to get a lot of ideas. "

Linus Pauling

Well I can tell you this; if you don't do it you won't be a big business for long. The fact is that in the days of pre-civilization, the person who started developing the wheel was considered an idiot!

This is why it is necessary to have team members bring five new ideas and present them at a team brain storming session. <u>Test your ideas</u>, first by open criticism and then by action; most will fail. However, the profit from your ideas that succeed; will far outweigh your losses from those that fails.

Just keep in mind that when you introduce the first "Brand" in a new category or niche, choose a <u>generic brand name</u> that are likely to become "the word" for the new category. This way you will be the top brand and the name used to describe all other products in your category.

Because, that means that every mention of the category is advertising for you!

On a final note, then <u>don't fall into the trap</u> of trying to "benchmark" your product or service in relativity to your competitors. Don't compare your products or services with theirs, it is futile and does not win in the long run.

Stick with being the first or original, it has worked for Coca Cola. Because, marketing is not about products it is all about customer perceptions.

If you are not the first in a category, then just create a new category or a sub-category in which you can be the first. A savvy entrepreneur will look for new niches in which the "first or leader" is nearly unknown. That niche and its leader is a "sitting duck", for a shock and awe marketing ambush.

Because, it is not just about being first in a niche; it is about being first in the minds and perceptions of the customer base!

Confirm

*An insider knows
what a business
needs today. An
outsider can tell
what it will need
tomorrow!*

Dan Sommer

When you learn something new, forget what you knew before. Try everything, but do it fast.

As mentioned in the "Dominate" chapter; 70% of customers, who take their business elsewhere, do it because of a lack of communication.

Therefore the "Confirm" phase is where you make your customers and all your prospects know who you are or what your brand or business is all about…

This can be done by sending unexpected letters in which you thank them personally for being your customer. Or that you regularly send them relevant info through your email newsletter list etc.

It can also be done by sending small but attention grapping gifts, with your name or logo on it along with a "bold" statement or slogan. Be creative and daring when you do this!

However a better way will be to write a new booklet or article and distribute it to your existing customers and everyone else on your email list. This is one of the most effective ways of marketing yourself and your business. Being an author is perceived by people

When I wrote the SD Agent in 2004, it was the first (SD) Surveillance Detection manual, which was available to the private sector. At that time I was neither the best known person in SD, nor known as a field expert in SD. However, today I am known as the leading expert, and the SD Specialist is still a top selling SD manual.

See: www.dansommer.biz

as synonymous with being an authority; hence the word authority is derived from author.

Most people erroneously believe that business books are written to earn money from them. However, this is far from the reality of business publishing. You write a business book because it is the most efficient and economic way to market your expertise to a large-scale market and create brand recognition for your business.

Most importantly, writing your own book will immediately establish you as a "perceived authority" in your field of business.

As soon as you have written it, then have it featured in the newspapers related to your target markets and contact television and radio news stations and offer to give interviews. Most people are reluctant or afraid to try this, because they think they are not important enough, or they feel unsure if their material is good enough for the news etc.

However, the fact is that no matter how little you know about a subject, there is always someone who knows less about it. I am not suggesting that you should write a book about a subject in which you have little or no experience.

My point is that even if you don't consider yourself an expert, you can be certain that to a lot of people your knowledge is already at the expert level.

The TV and Radio stations are having a constant battle to have fresh ideas and stories to cover and fresh faces to interview. Most Radio stations and many TV stations are broadcasting 24 hours a day, 365 days a year… and believe me; they are hard pressed to fill that airtime up with fresh and relevant material.

So go and get yourself interviewed and get some free advertisement and marketing from it, from which you will be able to reach new prospects and customers for free. But you will also find that at the same time you are attracting new customers, you will also re-attract your present customers.

Because every one of them who are viewing or listening; will immediately turn to their family or peers and say: hey I know him, that's the guy from company x that provides what we are using in department x. This creates a feeling of belonging to an elite user group and establishes pride in the customer. Thus, it further confirms your status as "their expert" on the matter!

On a final note, then keep your best customers in mind during the interview, and mention them in a positive way as an excellent example of how smart businesses are incorporating your expertise into better serving their customers. Now you have just advertised your own expertise as well as your clients business for free. By doing that you have not just flattered your client, but more importantly you have "cemented" them into your client fold.

> ## *"The greatest problem with communication is the illusion that it has been accomplished."*
> *George Bernard Shaw*

Keep the above quote in mind and remember that you are never finished communicating with your clients and prospects.

In business, communication is an ongoing and continuous process. However, it is also highly important to avoid being a "spammer" or one of those annoying callers, who just call and waste other people's time. Your customers are persons too and we all dislike, when someone send us to much commercial communications.

So make sure all your communications are short, relevant and to the point, which means you have to provide information that is relevant to your clients life or business.

If you prefer to call your business customers or prospects, then do it early in the morning, preferably in the first two office hours of business. Because, this is the time were people are in their office and more importantly they are fresh in, and you want to be the first person they talk to that day.

As we all know from running our businesses then there is nearly always something, which does not go according to the plan. There is almost always something or someone that comes up, which needs our immediate attention and that adds on to our work load and thus increases our stress level.

So the further into your customer's business day you call, the less chance there is that he will appreciate your call, and the time and effort you put into it. Most likely he will primarily pay attention to the time your call took away from his already busy schedule.

This is a prelude to failure, because the key to effective communication is to ensure that at the end of it, your customer or prospect is left with a positive image of you in his mind.

Therefore all your communications should be positive, understanding and offer solutions and ideas freely; then the sales will follow. If you call later in the day then you are getting closer to lunch and most businessmen are usually in a hurry to get things finished off before lunch.

Thus they are likely to "see" your sales call as an annoying interruption and will be brief and in a negative mode versus a positive sales mode.

The same accounts for calling customers in the afternoon; where businesses are trying to get urgent tasks completed before the end of the day. Most business people and managers are also frequently attending business meetings during this period, and are still trying to catch up.

So use the mornings to your advantage.

On a final note, then this is obviously primarily valid in the standard western marketplace, but could be entirely different in other cultures; such as for instance Latin America, where much of the business is conducted in the afternoon and in the evenings usually following a business dinner.

Overcome

Failure is prelude to success!

Dan Sommer

Accept this fact and continue with your business, because on an average each US millionaire has had 3.5 bankruptcies. Just think of entrepreneurs like Donald Trump, Richard Branson and Bill Bartman, they are multi-millionaires / billionaires today, because they did not let failure stop them!

Success is great and you can learn a lot from analyzing the successes of successful people and their businesses. But you will learn a lot faster and better, if you first study their failures. Failure is not just a ruthless teacher it is also the best teacher you can ever get; in life and in business.

Learning from your failures, got you from infant to teenager with little trouble. You would never have learned to crawl, walk or ride a bicycle, if you had allowed failure to stop you. Instead you just picked yourself up and with either a grin on your face or tears in your eyes, you tried again and again until you succeeded.

It was not before you reached your teens, that you became aware of what other people think about you and how you present yourself among them. And from that day, you started developing an "unnatural" fear of failure.

Overcoming that fear and learning to ignore your fear and its "arguments" is the key to success or failure.

If you can show me a successful business man or company, that has not had any failures in the last twelve months, then I am sure I can instead show you a person or company that is stagnant and in the process of dying!

To fail is to repeat a failure!

Dan Sommer

Success comes from repeated attempts, the more you try, the better your chance of success. This is a fact of evolution as well as in business. However, merely trying again after a failure is not the solution.

You will have to stop and assess the situation in detail before you try again. You need to find out what went wrong, when, how and why?

Dissect your last business plan and your entire operation, find out where the faults were made and find the solution to those faults; then try again. If you merely keep trying, without knowing what went wrong the first time (or the second time), then you are only going to repeat the process that let to failure.

This is the time for gut wrenching honesty and self criticism. Where exactly did you go wrong? Avoid blaming it on others or the market etc that is not solution finding, that's excuses. This year a common excuse for the failure of US based companies is to "blame" the high gasoline prices, as the reason why customers did not show up as expected…

That's an excuse and a lame excuse! Yes prices of gasoline are soaring but the sales volume of gasoline has gone up in 2007 and 2008, and so has the sale of gas-sucking vehicles such as SUV's. The price of gasoline is high, that is a fact, but it has not affected customers in such ways that they stay more home than before!

So do not look for external excuses, search for and <u>find the internal reasons</u> for the failures.

- Was the failure due to personnel reasons?

- Did you underestimate the work that had to be done?

- Did you or your employees not try hard enough?

- Were you or they simply just unwilling to work hard and committed during the start up process?

- Was there a lack of genuine passion in you or your personnel?

- In short, was it a personnel problem?

Well if so… then it is your "failure" because you did the hiring, you were the "Captain" aboard the ship. So discipline and examples were yours to set, and you obviously failed.

Good! Now that you know it, you can change it and Overcome.

Find the solution to the problems by addressing the issues that you have found. If personnel were the problem, then did you fail during recruitment? Did the persons mislead you, or do you attract or hire the wrong type of persons?

If you were the original source of the mistake, then accept responsibility so you can learn from your mistakes and then move on. If it was skills you were lacking, then take courses in the skill in which you failed, study and learn; then implement your new knowledge to find out where you went wrong.

If it is you, that attract the wrong kind of people, then outsource the hiring process to a recruitment agency etc. Dissect all problems honestly, then find the solution and implement it, no matter how hard it hurts your ego. Then go out and try it again.

This of course relates to all the other fields were you found out that you have failed, such as; production, services, marketing, selling, planning, expansion, development etc. Simply follow the same format as described in the personnel issue; Dissect the problem honestly, find the solution and implement it; no matter if it hurts your ego. Then go market your business again.

The fact is that near all problems in business are due to the human-fault factor, rarely is failure due to technical problems. Because, there is almost always an obvious solution to a technical problem and the solution can therefore near always be purchased with relative ease.

Of cause the solution could be too expensive which means your financial planning was obviously faulty, because if it is not possible to finance a solution to your technical problem; then your business concept is clearly bad.

For human factor problems, the best solution is often to educate, train and most importantly to decentralize the service processes and decision makings.

Please, notice that I wrote decentralize, not downsize; you cannot downsize and grow!

This is a fact many large corporations have learned the hard way, during the last ten years. So many mergers and acquisitions have been started by layoffs and immediate attempts to prune the corporate tree. Statistics and business analysis shows that the vast majority of mergers fail to meet the expectations and plans.

Regardless of this fact downsizing seems to be a common failure in today's business world; maybe because the board or owners are desperate to show a quick fix to their economical problems. But the fact is that experience has shown it to be a temporary fix only, and a bad one even for that.

If your sales are falling, then there are so many other things you should be doing, rather than fixate on laying off staff. Very often sales can be increased by hiring more sales staff and retraining and <u>motivating the entire sales force</u>.

However, there are good arguments for layoffs, especially when productivity is down. The key to success though, is to only lay off the unproductive members of the staff and filling their positions speedily, with new and motivated staff.

If sales figures or rather the lack of them is found to be the problem, then very often the problem is not just with the sales-force; but rather with the marketing methods and message.

> *"Your most*
> *unhappy customers*
> *are your greatest*
> *source of learning."*
> *Bill Gates*

To fix your current marketing problems all you have to do is <u>go through the AIDCO process</u> again and this time, change your ways and implement the ideas I gave you during the Advertising, Inform and Dominate chapters!

Keep Bill Gates quote in mind and go out and ask your current customers, what you can do better for them. Then go and visit your former customers and ask them how they felt you failed them. You will near always be surprised by their answers. But those answers are the keys to successfully turning your business around. So don't be afraid of it and remember to keep a positive and open mind to their complaints and advices.

The fact with everything in business is; that if you don't try, you will never know if it works. Thus take a chance on new ideas; just be ready to cut your losses if the product or service does not sell as planned. But before you cut it away, ask your customers if you can improve and adapt your service or product to better suit their needs.

Always remember that it is not your ideas, products or services that makes your business a success; it is your clients money!

Keep that fact in mind when you assess the answers to your inquiry. And keep in mind that it is often easier to scrap a business and start a new, than to change an unsuccessful business into a successful business. This is an unfortunate fact that many existing corporations and old style companies have failed to realize.

However, this fact is what gives entrepreneurial "upstarts" a growing market full of global opportunities. Because <u>entrepreneurs love challenges</u> and new ideas, and they are not afraid of taking chances.

<u>Too many</u> business owners and corporate boards <u>are too worried</u> about their status in society, to do what is right for their businesses. Thus, they continue to trot along the old trail and hope that things will change for the better. But the fact is; the "good old" times don't come back, because they were the <u>old times</u>!

The fact is that you are not doing yourself, your employees or the community any favors by trying to fight a futile battle. To do what is right in any given situation, is always better than being loyal!

To put this matter in context, then I will use a fire as a metaphor; "when you blow at a smoldering fire, you quickly get a brighter and hotter fire; unfortunately, it also means it will burn out faster and soon leave you with cold ashes."

To keep a fire burning bright, it needs more than a fresh supply of oxygen; it needs plenty of fresh firewood or fuel. This is the same in any business. Yes you can ignite the passion in the company staff. Yes you can market harder. Yes you can push for more sales and invest more money. And yes your business will likely appear brighter.

However, unless you have <u>an influx of new and fresh ideas</u> and products to offer to your customers; then your business will just burn out faster!

Thus, the overcome factor of the AIDCO process, symbolizes the need all businesses have for continued <u>growth, innovation and differentiation</u>. Being a growing and innovative business with a focus on differentiation, means you will make mistakes, whether you are a single entrepreneur or a large company.

The real secret in business is; that it is not the businesses that make no mistakes that succeed. Those business entrepreneurs that succeed are those **who are not afraid** to make mistakes.

However, they are also ruthlessly effective in recognizing, accepting and overcoming those mistakes.

Thus, as a true entrepreneur you either remake your business continuously, or launch a new idea and build a new successful business. As a true entrepreneur you will have to base your business plan on constant innovation, but you also have to ensure that you don't just innovate but also differentiate your products, your services and your marketing.

And the key is to have a passion for what you do and that passion must be transferable from you to your entire staff. Your passion must be epidemic and spread to your personnel and customers like a forest fire on a windy day.

The AIDCO Marketing Manual by Dan Sommer

It's AIDCO Time

During your reading of this book I hope that your mind have been opened up to new ideas and you will have realized that you need to learn new skills, obtain fresh talent and keep your mind open in today's innovative business world.

Without a doubt, you should now realize that AIDCO marketing is an extremely effective strategy for any small business. Since the majority of small businesses do not have a "large" advertising budget. It thus makes more sense to invest your passion, effort and time, in order to reap the full rewards of a <u>low cost but hard hitting</u> marketing strategy like AIDCO.

What you will gain from your AIDCO marketing campaign, will multiply or at least equal what you put into it. If you do not invest the passion, effort or time, then you will neither reap the rewards. Thus a successful AIDCO marketing campaign is an ongoing process, which consists of more than just one strategy or tactic.

Because the worst number in any marketing plan or sales process is ONE. You cannot afford to focus on only one direction of attack; you must "surround" your clients with your AIDCO marketing plan. A tactic is merely a way to win a battle, whereas a strategy is the way to win the war!

And in business you are literally in war with your competitors and you need to blast your competitors of your clients map, with your new <u>shock and awe AIDCO strategy</u>.

To conclude this chapter and the manual, then when you start to design and implement your AIDCO marketing strategy; remember to think outside the box constantly and keep innovation and differentiation, as a key component of your AIDCO marketing process. **And do not think you can start tomorrow; You Must Start Right Now!**

To those readers who just wanted a quick "cheat-sheet" type book; then I will end this final chapter by a quote that says it all…

"Learning is not compulsory, But neither is survival."

W. Edwards Deming,
management consultant

Thanks for reading my AIDCO Marketing Manual. **Now Go and Implement it!**

And implementation of AIDCO is not just for business but also for your professional career and your personal life. So to get you started I have included 3 Quick Step Guides to getting your:

1. Personal Life
2. Professional Career
3. Business Success

On the fast track to success!

1. Life Coaching for Masters of Brilliant Achievements

Your success and it's less desirable counterpart failure, are both caused by ourselves, not by anyone or anything else!

From the time you reached adulthood, you and only you are responsible for all your actions, thoughts, emotions as well as the position's you hold in your life.

You are exactly where you aimed to be! You did not get to where you are today by accident, you caused the affects that placed you in the exact situation that you are in right now. That is a fact, whether you like it or not.

The only exception is of cause if someone actually caused a physical action or accident to occur to you. Obviously if you were run-over by a drunken driver while you were walking down the pavement towards work, then obviously you are not responsible for being in the hospital or any disabilities you may suffer from the accident.

However, you do choose how you mentally allow the accident to affect your physical recovery and your future emotional state.

However, for 99% of the readers then there are no more excuses to hide behind, besides you are only fooling yourself. So, if you are looking for excuses for your failures and any under-achievements you are experiencing, then just close this book and go whine to someone else. Better yet, go and find personal or motivational counseling.

So, if you really want to achieve success and are prepared to accept responsibility for your actions, thoughts and current position in life, then this book by Dan Sommer, will take you towards your success.

I guarantee you that if you follow the message and action plans given on my webpage www.dansommer.biz, then you will achieve your goals and see your vision come through in less than three years. In addition, I can also guarantee you that your life will have improved significantly in just three months.

So let us not waster more time, for time is precious and it is the only "thing" that we can never increase. Every day lost is a day lost forever. So, without further delays, it is time for entrepreneurial action!

Achieving What You Want In Life

To achieve what you want in life, there is fundamentally only 4 points you need to focus on. Because that way you will achieve the most from your efforts, and thus achieve your life coaching goals.

1. First: Do more of the things that you value the most and which provides you with the greatest emotional reward and financial gain.

2. Second: Do less of things that de-motivate you and take time away from the tasks that you value higher. In other words, start doing less of

the things that does not bring you closer to your goals and values.

3. Third: Do new things and learn new skills that you are not doing today, but which are in direct alignment with your values, and would be helpful in getting you closer to your goals.

4. Fourth: Do not do things that are contrary to your values and which distances you from your goals. Evaluate all your behaviors and tasks and aim to remove those that does not align with your values or bring you closer to your goals and vision. If you cannot eliminate all of these tasks immediately them refer to point two immediately.

Success is best achieved by taking actions that increases your productivity and your financial income. However, "Total Success" will only be achieved when you do that, while at the time decreasing your working hours spent on professional tasks. Then add those hours you are saving to the hours spent on personal tasks and goals.

Working harder and longer never solves any "real" problems or helps achieve any long-term goals. It only offers temporary results and a short-term increase in productivity and financial gain. However, such solutions eventually create long-term losses.

Working smarter while increasing your time off from professional tasks will boost your physical energy as well as your mental ability to be innovative and creative. Physical Energy and Mental Ability are the two fundamental pillars of continuous success in all businesses as well as personal lives.

By reducing, the times spend on professional tasks and increasing the times spend on personal tasks; you will both raise your personal motivation, and increase your perceived status among your peers and customers. Both of which are essential for the achievement of permanent success.

2. Get a Successful Career by Simple Career Planning

Once you have come to realize what your genuine desire is, and have ensured that it is consistent with your personal values. Then all you have to do is simply to move in the obvious direction that leads towards your desire.

The 3 Pillars of Career Success

You can start by reading several self-help books or listen to motivational cd's and subscribe to career related newsletters. There are loads of information out there about the right way and the ultimate solution etc.

Hey, I have even written some of them and I also publish a newsletter and I would be glad to have you buy them and subscribe to them. But, you are really no different from any of the so-called Guru's or from me.

In fact you have all the same potentials and unless you are mentally or physically impaired, then you can make you career as success story all by yourself, if you so desire. All you have to do is learn and follow the Three Pillars of Career Success.

- ✓ Point 1. Nothing happens until something moves

- ✓ Point 2. Become internally who you want to be externally

- ✓ Point 3. It is not the journey, but the destination that is important

Career Coaching is simply Career Planning... with Guidance, Help and Motivation... There are never any "quick solutions" to life's many problems, including career problems. There are only gradual improvements.

When you search for solutions, you are wasting precious time and energy, which you could instead have used to make several small but highly important improvements.

Following a simple plan of incremental improvements, such as the "Six Step" SECURE career coaching strategy, will always prove to be far more efficient and profitable than any "quick solution" fix as frequently advertised.

Every journey and career move, begins with a small step and continues step by step until you reach your destination. However, once you are there and have enjoyed the sights and experiences, you will feel the urge to go to somewhere better.

That is the natural journey of life and it is a journey that never ends, and which consists of many different phases and travels, which will take you to various places.

To effectively move forward in your career, you will have to keep looking forward and you will have to regularly look up towards your points of destination. However, in order for you to arrive successfully, you will have to look most at what is directly in front of you. This is essential so that you can steer around any obstacles and avoid any pitfalls.

Thus you should only look up at your point of destination, in order to keep your general point of direction.

The problem most people have with their career and life is that they look to the past for causes and to the future for solutions. Thus they go through life and career with one leg stuck in the past and the other leg ahead in the future. As a result... they are "urinating" on today's opportunities!

If your daily actions are build upon a "future vision" that is based on some "utopian" idea. And if your current re-actions to challenges and problems are based on finding causes in your past, and what has happened. Then you will be using those causes as excuses for your current problems and recent failures. Well... is it then really a mystery, why your current career situation seems stained with "yellow"?

Referring back to Point 1.

"Nothing happens until something moves", then that simply mean that if you genuinely want change your career or specific parts of it, then you need to take action. You will need to move your life and your career in a new direction today! Planning and research is good, but too much planning and research is just an excuse for delaying actions due to fear of failure.

Referring back to Point 2.

"Become internally who you want to be externally", that that simply mean that you have to have the self-discipline to change yourself and your life. Do not allow yourself to fall into the trap in which you pretend to yourself and others that you do not know what to do or how to do it. You already know what you need to do and you know how you can learn to do it, SO STOP Wasting Time and Just DO IT!

Referring back to Point 3.

"It is not the journey, but the destination that is important", then that simply mean that whether your journey is constantly fun and exciting, or at times seems long and hard. Then it is important to realize that it is not the specific phases of the journey that is important, it is the arrival at your chosen destination that is important.

Your Career Development:

Every choice you make affects your life and career, whether for good or for bad depends entirely upon you. You will know exactly what choices to make, if you just allow your values to lead you towards your goals. Start by focusing on what you have achieved in your career and you will soon find yourself feeling good about yourself.

When you feel good about yourself then other people will also feel good about you. Your career will only move in the direction you lead it and it will only move at a pace equal to the time and energy you put into it.

I guarantee, that if you follow the message and action plans outlined in this book and on my webpage www.dansommer.biz, then you will achieve your goals and see your vision come through in less than three years. In addition, I can also guarantee you that your career will have improved significantly in just three months.

So let us not waster more time, for time is precious and it is the only "thing" that we can never increase. Every day lost is a day lost forever. So, without further delays, it is time for entrepreneurial action!

3. Marketing Your Security Business Effectively

Are you facing the dilemma of either having to spend a lot of money on a paid marketing program or call it quits on your security business? Because, there is a set of basic, fundamental things you MUST do to succeed with your Security Business.

Press Releases are one of the best ways to promote your security consultancy business in a professional, yet affordable manner.

Getting free Publicity through issuing press releases is by far the most cost-effective marketing tool available to the small and medium sized security businesses. This due to the fact that the cost is mainly limited to the time it takes you to compose your press release.

Why are press releases so important in the overall marketing strategy that all major security businesses issue them regularly? Because, press releases is the only part of a marketing strategy that builds credibility for you and your security business.

Many security niches have innovative "up-start companies" that are relatively unknown. If such new businesses are to gain a foothold and even an edge over their competition, then it is essential that they build credibility through publicity in "main stream" Medias.

To begin with, it is important to understand that even though press releases are an important part of the marketing strategy. Then a press release is not an advertising and nor is it a sales letter. A press release is a marketing tool disguised as a news broadcast.

To ensure your security business press release is both news worthy and professional in appearance, then you will need to adhere to the 10 PR rules. To ensure your security press release is both news worthy and professional, then you will need to adhere to these ten rules:

1. Make sure the information is newsworthy, it must include news.

2. Tell the audience that the information is intended for them and why they should continue to read it.

3. Start with a brief description of the news, then distinguish who announced it, and write it is third person.

4. Ask yourself, "How are people going to relate to this and will they be able to connect with my marketing point?"

5. Make sure the first 10 words of your release are effective and relative to your business niche, as they are the most important.

6. Avoid excessive use of adjectives and fancy language, plain niche talk.

7. Focus on the facts not on your business.

8. Provide full contact information: such as the individual to contact, address, phone, fax, email, Web site address, Skype. The more methods the better.

9. Don't issue your PR until you have something substantial to report on or comment on before you issue a press release.

10. Make it as easy as possible for media representatives to do their jobs, so include links to sites with more information on your business and the topic of your press release.

If the above ten rules have not already inspired you to start writing your first press release and you still feel a little unsure about how to proceed... Then, don't worry. Because, there is solution that will help you create professional press releases quickly and easily namely the New "Press Release Pro" - Creator Software, by Dan Sommer.

With the new PressReleasePro you will quickly and easily be able to "Maximize Your Media Exposure" and increase your websites search engine traffic by using the New PressReleasePro Creator software when creating your own press releases. What you can do with the Press Releases you create with the PressReleasePro.

- ✓ You can send them to your local medias - newspaper, radio, TV, etc.
- ✓ Send them to press release submission services for quick media exposure.
- ✓ Send them to industry specific websites that are relevant to your business.
- ✓ Upload them to your website to add credibility to your business.
- ✓ Use the press releases to increase your search engine ranking
- ✓ Use the press releases as a marketing tool and thus increase your sales

You cannot "get by" in business without these PR skills; they are 100% necessary for your business success. The New PressReleasePro, is a simple application or "exe" script, that you will soon use to create your own Professional looking Press Releases. You can generate an infinite number of Press Releases and send them to online and offline Medias and post them on any web page you want.

I once read a statement by a great marketer:
"There are 3 kinds of people in the world:

Those that MAKE THINGS HAPPEN...

Those that WATCH Things Happen...

and Those that SAY "What Happened?"

So Make it Happen Today, and do it For Your Own Sake!

Dan Sommer

www.DanSommer.Biz

P.S. If you are still not quite sure where to start or feel slightly uneasy about it, then just keep in mind that this is how your competitor feels as well. So just get to it… Right Now!

P.P.S. Don't be shy, just call or email me if you want to make sure you get your marketing right. After all, my coaching and consulting fees are far less than the salary you will command as a successful entrepreneur.

P.P.P.S. If you need help getting your career or business started on a track to success, then simply read the next chapter…

Dan Sommer

Dan Sommer is a successful Business Consultant who also provides Career Coaching to security entrepreneurs and small business managers. He teaches a line of Success seminars to small businesses and entrepreneurs, with a focus on differentiation and innovation in both Marketing and Business Management.

As a consultant Dan has coached and mentored more than 300 persons from 15 different countries. He has completed dozens of courses in various topics such as; security, protection and counter-terrorism and has Diplomas in Marketing & Business Management.

Dan Sommer is co-founder of Global Executive Outreach a UK based Risk & Crisis Management Consultancy with international clientele and operations in countries such as Djibouti, Egypt, Japan, Lebanon, Oman, Saudi Arabia, South Korea, UK and Yemen.

Dan Sommer is the author of:

The AIDCO Marketing Manual – 2008
Terrorist Modus Operandi – 2008
The Website Video Success Manual – 2008
The Social Site Directory – 2008

The K&R Crisis Response Manual – 2007
The Video Marketing Guide – 2007
The Tactical PPC Marketing Guide – 2007
The Press Release Pro Manual – 2007
The SECURE Career Manual – 2006
The DARE Life Manual – 2006
The Modern Entrepreneur – 2005
The Terrorist Planning Process – 2005
The Surveillance Detection Specialist – 2004
SATOD the Warriors Bible – 2001

Dan currently acts as the Director of Business Development at GEO – Global Executive Outreach Ltd in UK and Global Executive Outreach S.A.L. in Lebanon. He was the Chairman of the World Federation of Bodyguards from 2000 to 2008, and has a security and protection career spanning more than 20 years. He has active experience as an operator and instructor, in military, security, close protection, counter assault teams and surveillance detection operations.

He has been designing training programs for security companies and police departments since 1994, and has instructed courses world-wide for security officers, bodyguards, police officers, counter assault teams and surveillance detection units. Dan has worked on security and protection projects in several countries including: Denmark, Djibouti, Egypt, England, Hong Kong, Iceland, Macau, Mexico, Nigeria, Northern Ireland, Oman, Wales and Yemen.

Dan Sommer was born in Copenhagen, Denmark in 1967. He left Denmark in 1988 and moved to Iceland, since then he has also lived in Mexico and England. Today he lives in the beautiful city of Reykjavik, which is the capitol of Iceland and the Northernmost of capitols in the world.

More importantly though, then Reykjavik is also one of the most efficient business environments in the world. In the last decade Iceland, a country that only has a tiny population of 310,000; has climbed from global obscurity into being a high ranking contender on the top of the worlds businesses (2007 consensus):

- Iceland is 2nd in Business Efficiency

- Iceland is 3rd in Gross Domestic Product - Per capita

- Iceland is 5th in Purchasing Power Parity - Per capita

- Iceland is 7th on the World Competitiveness Board

Even with its tiny population Iceland is the innovational leader is several fields of eco-green and environmentally friendly energy systems, such as: geo-thermal energy and hydrogen fuel development.

Iceland is also a leader in medical research of DNA and genetics as well as in the generic medicine industry. In the "old Europe" and especially in countries such as the UK and in Scandinavia, the Icelandic businesses are well known as "the" innovators of the retail sector.

Icelandic businesses innovation strategies have turned around own several world known retail brands such as:

Debenhams, Hamleys, Zara, Topshop, Karen Millen, All Saints, The Shoe Studio, Iceland, Booker, Warehouse, Whistles, Oasis, Dorothy Perkins, Evans, Coast, House of Fraser, Frasers, Howells, Dickins & Jones, Rackhams, Army & Navy, Jenners, Beatties, Magasin Du Nord, Illum, Merlin, Julian Graves, Whittard of Chelsea, Goldsmiths, Woodward Foodservice, Mappin & Webb, Linea, Howick and Therapy. As well as entertainment brands such as Lazytown, Bjork, and Sigurros.

Dan Sommer's Consulting Services

- Are you planning to start a Small Business?
- Do you need help creating a business plan?
- Do you need help creating a Marketing Plan?
- Do you need help setting Business Guidelines?

Then you are not alone... Because the majority of persons starting a New Business, usually have a prior career in which they were specialist's in their specific field; and therefore do not have any direct business and marketing experience.

This is specifically true in the Private Security Industry, were near all new companies are started by persons with a prior active career in either Law Enforcement or Armed Forces; and thus naturally does not have direct business and marketing experience.

However, you are on the right track because you are looking for assistance, you realize that you will professional help with making your new business a success and to secure the retirement plan you deserve.

Small Business Consulting Approach:

Dan Sommer consultancy services; focus on small businesses. I prefer to work with businesses that are small, lean, fast paced and flexible to the needs of their clients.

The business manager/s and/or owner/s should have the ability to react quickly to changes in their business sector and have the will to exploit these new opportunities. I guarantee you that I will live up to the same requirements.

Why work with Dan Sommer as your consultant? Well you have just read my AIDCO Marketing Manual, so you already know that I know what I am talking about and you know that I have the experience and knowledge that you need.

But there are other good reasons, such as: I am Faster: I will focus on your business needs and together we will find the right solutions fast and securely. Because you and your staff do not have the time it requires to work on your problems full time.

I have the knowledge and experience that you need, in order to meet your business commitments. When we combine your insight and my experience and unbiased view; your business will succeed.

International Experience: Because I have worked across continents with many companies in different sectors, from Europe, Asia and Central America.

I bring knowledge and experience in many specific areas of business: including business management, business planning, marketing planning, personnel management and security operations.

I also bring specialized security skills that very likely does not exist within your company, and I can teach you and your staff these skills.

I can and help you implement those new services, if they match your business plan. Together we can solve your business obstacles and find solutions to any challenges and create for innovative ideas.

Cost effective solution:

I am here when you need me, and I can come to you when and if it is needed, in accordance with our consultancy agreement.

Together we get the challenges solved and the problems eliminated, and then I have finished my task, and thus there is no more fees from my side and you don't sit up with an "extra" employee.

Using a consultant is much more cost effective than having to hire someone to do the same task. I will be on your virtual staff without you having to invest time and finances in permanent staff.

Small Business Consulting:

My Business Consulting services include advice on starting a small business, writing marketing and business plans, making a business analysis, and management, marketing and business consulting.

✓ Writing a Business Plan: Writing a business plan should be thought of as creating a blueprint for success for your business. An effective business plan conveys a great story, weaving an exciting plan that captivates the reader. You want 50 pages of brilliant strategies and accurate statistics.

✓ Writing a Marketing Plan: Your marketing plan is your plan to bring your product or service to the market place. Marketing strategies match or transform your product or services to the needs of your customers. Good market research will uncover marketing ideas for new products or services that are not presently being met.

✓ Business Analysis: Before we start anything else we will together audit your current business status by completing a business analysis. This business analysis will show the strengths and weaknesses within your business. This will give us an excellent starting point for improving your business operations quickly.

What are the benefits of working with Dan Sommer?

The same "Nr-1" business rule applies in all business sectors, namely the need to do things faster than the competitors. With this need for doing things faster, you as a small security business manager or owner; need to learn the rules of business quickly or lose out to those who do.

You will therefore have to study for hours and hours each day, while still managing your business and all your other daily chores at the same time.

The Solution:

However, there is a better solution to accelerate your business learning, and that is to let Dan Sommer provide you with personal mentoring.

My business consultancy services usually involves, instruction combined with coaching and review of work assignments directly related to your business success.

The benefits:

The real benefit of my business consultancy services, is that there is nothing that speeds up the business process, like having a professional business consultant and coach.

You need a Consultant and Coach who is willing to teach you the exact needed processes and strategies in person. Learning from other's successes and mistakes, is ultimately one of the quickest and safest ways to learn.

Dan Sommer's MBA Coaching Programs

Dan Sommer offers personal coaching programs for independent security contractors and security business entrepreneurs. These programs are based upon Dan's personal experience in the security and protection industry and his successful manuals. Dan Sommer's *MBA* programs are an acronym for *Masters of Brilliant Achievements.*

Business Coaching

- Are you unable to grow your Business?
- Are your un-billed working hours increasing?
- Are you struggling to reach set business goals?
- Do you want more time and less stress?

Then you are not alone...

Because the majority of entrepreneurs and business managers feel trapped and overpowered by constantly having to tend to "urgent" and time consuming matters, which does not increase the business profits. They essentially spend so much time "turning out fires" that their own "fire" is slowly extinguished.

Business Coaching Approach:

Dan Sommer's Business Coaching services are focused on supporting small businesses in achieving success. I prefer to work with business managers who have a passion for their "industry" and are in charge of small, lean and fast paced businesses.

The business coached entrepreneur or business manager should have the ability and willingness to react quickly to changes in their business sector, as well as have the will to exploit these business opportunities. I guarantee you that I will live up to the same requirements.

Why work with Dan Sommer?

Because as your Business Coach I will: Keep you focused on what's important for your business, when you're feeling frustrated by the many time-robbers that arises daily in every business unless they are dealt with systematically.

Keep you focused on finding, setting and implementing strategies needed to improve the bottom line of your business, so you can keep the profit making balls rolling while doing what you enjoy.

Keep you honing the management skills you need in order to keep achieving the business successes you need and know you are really capable of achieving.

Keep you focused on daily attendance to the 3-Key Tasks that no entrepreneur or business manager can "afford" to delegate the responsibility for, as these 3-Key Tasks are fundamental to success.

Hold yourself accountable for what you say you'll do, so that things get done as they were planned and when they were planned.

The benefits:
The real benefit of my business coaching services, is that there is nothing that increases profits and business success the way that you will as a highly effective and passionate entrepreneur.

You need a business coach who is willing and able to encourage you to stick with the game plan, as well as motivate you to get the plan implemented, even in the adversity of obstacles and troubles.

In short I will help you regain the passion and fire that's been dwindling inside of you and restore the fun to you business life again, so you can return to being the successful you again!

> ## *"Does coaching work? Yes. Good coaches provide a truly important service. They tell you the truth when no one else will."*
>
> *Jack Welch*

Career Coaching

Why should you enroll in Dan Sommer's Career Coaching program? Because, near all of the Fortune 500 companies use coaching is because they know it is far more economical and efficient, to teach their personnel to learn how to solve their work problems and increase their strengths, rather than having to hire a consultant every time a problem comes up.

An in-house mentor will usually work well with technical problems and taught skills; but it takes a independent career coach to increase your personal performance, learning and problem solving abilities.

If your employer is not among the majority of the Fortune 500 companies, which use coaching programs, then you owe it to yourself to take charge of your own career and propel it forward with the help of a Career Coach.

"Between 25 percent and 40 percent of Fortune 500 companies use executive coaches"

Survey by The Hay Group, International

Why Is Career Coaching So Effective? Because it is all about your success. With Dan Sommer as your career coach, you can cut through the haze and reduce the pitfalls out of your career and pave your route with the focused efforts you need to move forward today.

If you are "working hard and confused" instead of "working smart and goal oriented", I can help you achieve your future today.

There are times in our lives where we need unbiased criticism and go-do-it motivation, so we can see ourselves for who we really are and where we are going. So if you are ready to move on with your career and achieve the status you know you deserve, then I am the right career coach for your needs.

If you want to live a life were every day is started with great expectation and every challenge is welcomed as an opportunity to grow; then success is your chosen road and the road to success starts today.

So What Is Career Coaching Exactly? Career coaching is really the goal of good management, that help you unfold your full potentials without limitations, so you can become who you really are.

Career coaching is an ongoing systematic process designed to get you to where you want to be, while achieving what you want to achieve.

Career coaching help you achieve your goals faster and more efficiently by holding your focus on the strategy and tactics that best serve you goals.

Career coaching helps you identify, clarify and achieve your real value goals and not just those goals that temporarily suits your agenda.

"Without a coach, people will NEVER reach their maximum capabilities"

Bob Nardelli (CEO of Home Depot)

What Coaching Process Do You Go Through with Dan Sommer? You will achieve what you want in your career, by following my tested and proven 6-step; SECURE career program:

What does SECURE stand for?

- ✓ **Survey your Position** – in this step you to create a strong personal foundation that allows you to observe yourself with clarity and strength, and define your dream career.

- ✓ **Explore your Options** – in the second step you will identify your personal strengths and weaknesses and how to use them to enter the career niche you have chosen.

✓ **Create your Game-Plan** - in the third step you formulate your tactics, strategy, and schedule needed to achieve your goals, this step defines your career plan in details.

✓ **Unfold your Potential** - in the fourth step you unfold your personal marketing plan with commitment, dedication and an ambitious focused drive towards your goal.

✓ **Reach your Objectives** - in step five you will have achieved your personal set career goal, you will now have identified your core values and have clarified your life.

✓ **Evaluate your position** – in step six you will be able to imagine new possibilities, evaluate your core values and true life goals, and thus you can fully explore your life.

According to a survey by Metrix Global (Nov. 2001) people who partner with professional coaches report a 529-788% return on investment in the areas of financial, career and overall emotional benefits.

The SECURE process:

Is based on your career needs, but will often last up to six months and consists of three monthly consultations plus emails. I will share with you my techniques, experiences and insiders know-how; I have used successfully to "open-doors", obtain contracts and propel my personal career forward.

If you are frustrated with the lack of responses when you send out resumes, the low salaries for the contracts you do receive, and tired of promises that never materialize about possible placements.

Then you will benefit immediately from my AIDCO marketing approach. The proven and tested AIDCO market manual is a free benefit, when you sign up for my SECURE career program and it's a secure market approach you will use for the rest of your life.

Life Coaching

What exactly is Life Coaching? Life coaching is not therapy or counseling, it is not about solving past crises or traumas. Life Coaching is about finding out where you are today and get you to where you want to be in the near future.

Life Coaching is about getting you to where you really want to be and have the happy life you deserve. Life Coaching with Dan Sommer is a supportive and confidential one-on-one relationship, focused on just one thing; your success.

As a Life Coach my aim is to help you stabilize your life, achieve your goals and enjoy a happy personal life. I will strategize with you to help you solve your problems and make the most of your life and opportunities.

"Who exactly seeks out a coach?

Winners who want even more out of life. "

Chicago Tribune

What Life Coaching Process Do You Go Through with Dan Sommer? You will achieve what you want in your life, by following the tested and proven 4-step DARE success program: What is DARE?

1. **Downsize your daily tasks** – take a step back and take a realistic look at both your work and your private life, and reassess them by assigning true values, anything that does not provide you with significant value should be cut off and eliminated. There is no value to time management that only save you minutes, what you need is life management. I will help you locate and realize your goals!

2. **Absorb from others** – if you want to succeed you need to learn to absorb and adopt other people's ideas, time, finances, energy, knowledge, contacts and success. When you let go of your ego you will realize that there are people who have already done what you are doing now, so stop pulling all the weight yourself and instead absorb strength from others. I will help you locate the resources that will ease your burden!

3. **Research what others have done** – to truly get ahead in your career and life you need to pass start before beginning; this may sound strange but never start anything from square-one, there is no need to start there, because 90% of what you are about to do have been done before. So build your next success on

existing ideas and the experiences from other people's failures. I will help you locate and implement the knowledge you need!

4. **Energize yourself every day** – to stay on top of your career and personal life you need to learn to take time off for yourself, to relax and rebuild your character and refresh your ideas. Most business failures started with hard work and ended with sheer exhaustion. Today almost everyone works too much and spend too much time on worthless task at work and at home. I will help you design your own life-energizing program!

During the DARE process you will experience a fundamental change in your life that will restore your joy and positive energy; this is a process which should never end, but instead become part of your life from this moment and until you retire permanently from this world.

From the day you start the DARE life style you will feel better every day, be more energetic and get more done. You will spend more time with your family and friends as well as having more time for yourself and your passions.

Not to mention that you will soon earn more money than you ever did before.

Let me ask you one final question:

If you could have the perfect life, would you choose the life you have now? If not then you know what you must do to change that answer!

My services are neither free nor cheap, but...

✓ What is the value of your business investment?

✓ What is the value of having a great career?

✓ What is the value of your personal happiness?

Pause for a moment and ponder...

Because, these are 3 questions you should seriously consider before taking the decision to improve your life immediately and permanently.

From a business point of view then it is very simple, you just need to calculate how much time, energy and money you have invested in your business, and how badly you want your investments to pay off.

From a personal point of view then it is also very simple, you just ask yourself if achieving your goals and dreams are worth the fee I charge!

Consulting Fees

My Consulting fees are based on providing my clients with immediate valuable knowledge and task assignments, which can be implemented immediately into their businesses.

Knowledge fuels success and knowledge plus direct advice on how to best apply the knowledge, is the focus of my security business consulting program.

Yet while I realize the immense value of my program, I also realize that many small or new businesses are operating on tight budgets, thus me fees are competitively and fairly priced.

Coaching Fees

My Coaching fees are based on providing my clients with true value and benefits for their money, while still keeping the fee low enough so that ordinary persons can afford my life coaching.

My fees are also based on that the entry level career focused individual can afford to build his career, with career coaching from the start.

Yet my fees are also fair representations of the time, energy and money I have invested in my life experience, management experience and education.

Dan Sommer's Life Coaching Fees

30-Day's - Life Coaching Program: This includes three, 45 minute private and confidential telephone coaching calls. During the program we will fast track my proven 5 step DARE Life coaching program, which I will help you implement for your personal Life success. Additionally the program includes two emails a week with "day after" reply support throughout the month. Fee only $249.

90-Day's - Life Coaching Program: This includes nine, 45 minute private and confidential telephone coaching calls. During the program we will point for point, follow my proven 5 step DARE Life coaching program, which I will help you implement for your personal Life success. Additionally the program includes two emails a week with "day after" reply support throughout the coaching period. Fee only $679.

Dan Sommer's Career Coaching Fees

30-Day's - Career Coaching Program: This includes three, 45 minute private and confidential telephone coaching calls. During the program we will fast track my proven 7 step SECURE security career coaching program, which I will help you implement for your career success. Additionally the program includes two emails a week with "day after" reply support throughout the month. Fee only $329.

90-Day's - Career Coaching Program: This includes nine, 45 minute private and confidential telephone coaching calls. During the program we will point for point, follow my proven 7 step SECURE security career coaching program, which I will help you implement for your career success. Additionally the program includes two weekly emails with "day after" reply throughout the coaching period. Fee only $879.

Dan Sommer's Business Consulting Fees

30-Day's - Business Consultancy Program: This includes three, 45 minute private and confidential telephone consultancy calls. During the program, we will fast track and implement my proven 7 step AIDCO Business Management & Marketing Program, which I will help you implement for your Business success. Additionally the program includes two weekly emails with "day after" reply throughout the month. Fee only $459

90-Day's - Business Consultancy Program: This includes nine, 45 minute private and confidential telephone consultancy calls. During the program we will point for point, follow my proven 7 step AIDCO Business Management & Marketing program, which I will help you implement for your Business success. Additionally the program includes two weekly emails with "day after" reply throughout the coaching period. Fee only $1199.

5-Day's - Intensive Onsite Business Consultancy Tutorial: This includes 20 hours of private and confidential tutorials/seminars. Consisting of 10 hours Intensive Business Consultancy sessions that follows my proven 7 step AIDCO Business and Marketing Program. And 10 hours Career Coaching sessions that follow my proven 7 step SECURE security career coaching program, which aims at making you a respected business leader. All 20 hours are delivered at your office or your choice of venue and you decide if your staff will participate. Fee only $4700.

If you wish to learn more from Dan Sommer:

Dan Sommer - Career Coach & Business Consultant
DanSommer@internet.is
Address: Bakkastadir 161 - 112 Reykjavik - Iceland
Office Tel US: +1 (202) 905-0439
Office Tel UK: +44 020 8133 9064
Office Tel DK: +45 36 95 98 19
Cell-phone IS: +354 663 0552
www.DanSommer.Biz and www.GEO-Ops.com

I am not the "Savior" of Small Businesses… I cannot guarantee you entry to "Business-Heaven".

But I can definitely prevent you from going to "Business-Hell"

Dan Sommer

Recommended Reading

Here Below you will find a short list of business and marketing books, which I not only have read, but also have tried and tested the tactics and strategies they describe. I have found these books to be among the great books of real value that I can fully recommend. Each of these books have given me part of the knowledge I used to establish my business success and create the AIDCO system!

Peters, Tom, *The Circle of Innovation*. New York: Alfred Knopf, 1997.

Peters, Tom, *Re-Imagine!*. London: Dorling Kindersley, 2003.

Welch, Jack & Welch, Suzy, *Winning*. New York: HarperCollins Publishers, 2005

Collins, Jim, *Good to Great*. London: Random House, 2001

Silbiger, Steven, *The 10-Day MBA*. London: Piatkus Books, 2005

Tracy, Brian, *Focal Point*. New York: AMACOM, 2005

Adamson, Allen, *BrandSimple*. New York: Palgrave Macmillian, 2006

Trout, Jack, *Differentiate or Die*. New York: John Wiley & Sons, 2000

Silber, Lee, *Self-Promotion for the Creative Person*. New York: Three Rivers Press, 2001

Ries, Al & Trout, Jack, *The 22 Immutable Laws of Marketing*. New York: HarperCollins Publishers, 1994

Gitomer, Jeffrey, *Little Red Book of Selling*. Ausin: Bard Press, 2005

Kennedy, Dan, *No B.S. Wealth Attraction for Entrepreneurs*. Irvine: Entrepreneur Media, 2006

Kennedy, Dan & Glazer, Bill & Skrob, Robert, *The Official Get Rich Guide to Information Marketing*. Irvine, Entrepreneur Media, 2007

Hopkins, Claude, *My Life in Advertising and Scientific Advertising*. Chicago: NTC Business Books, 1998

Spence, Gerry, *How to Argue and Win Every Time*. New York: St. Martins Press, 1995

Sutton, Garrett, *The ABC's of Writing Winning Business Plans.* New York: Warner Books, 2005

Johnson, Spencer, *Who Moved My Cheese.* London: Random House, 2000

Carlson, Richard, *Don't Sweat the Small Stuff.* New York: Hyperion, 1997

Covey, Stephen, *Principle Centered Leadership.* New York: Simon & Schuster, 1992

Hill, Napoleon, *Think and Grow Rich.* Minneapolis: Filiquarian Publishing, 2005

Whitcomb, Susan Britton, *30-Day Job Promotion.* Indianapolis: JIST Publishing, 2008

Tepper, Ron, *Become a Top Consultant.* New York: John Wiley & Sons, 1985

Forsyth, Patrick, *Smart Things to Know About Consultancy.* Oxford: Captsone Publishing, 2002

Lok, Dan, *Creativity Sucks.* New York: Morgan James Publishing, 2006